LIVE

C⚡NNECTIONS

Virtual Facilitation for High Engagement and Powerful Learning

FREDRIK **FOGELBERG** | JUDE **TAVANYAR** *Et al*

ISBN 978-90-823504-0-1

10 9 8 7 6 5 4 3 2 1

This book is available to order online.
www.createspace.com/5408192
www.amazon.com/dp/9082350408
www.nomadicibp.com

Illustrations by Kees Smits
www.speedcartooning.nl

Typesetting and cover design Tambourine Design
www.tambourinedesign.co.uk

Nomadic
International
Business
Psychology

www.nomadicibp.com

PREFACE

···

A Word from Fredrik Fogelberg and Jude Tavanyar

From Fredrik ...

This book has been written by a team, but I would like to start with a personal story. On a dreary autumn day late in 2009, in the middle of the dramatic financial crisis which brought several banks to bankruptcy, I was visiting a client in Antwerp in Belgium for an executive coaching session. My client Louis*, was a senior manager at Fusion*, a global high tech company. This is what he shared with me as our conversation started: 'Do you know what, the Board has forced a total travel ban. I'm not even allowed to take the train to see my boss in Paris anymore.'

He was appalled at the prospect of having to communicate entirely virtually with all his peers, superiors and reports. He did not believe it was possible to build and maintain sensible working relationship virtually and he would also miss his frequent short trips that made a nice break in the weekly routine. On the train back home to the Netherlands, I reflected on what Louis had said. I came to the conclusion that the deep economic crisis would probably affect many other organisations to take similar drastic measures to lower cost and increase efficiency. Given the rapid evolution of communication technology, working together across distance was well on its way to becoming easier and more commonplace. I decided that there was a clear learning need here for people like Louis who were forced to make the transition from collocated to remote working and weren't as excited as their children might be to use technology to communicate.

Sven Cune joined me shortly after this and we embarked on a journey exploring various web platforms, testing them within our team, with friends and with patient clients. We made many mistakes and by trial and error, slowly developed a style, etiquette and set of habits that made working remotely not only a necessity but a joy. During a workshop with Dr Ghislaine Caulat, Founder and Director of Black Gazelle Consulting Ltd and Associate Client Director at Ashridge School of Management, I made the shift from seeing virtual teamwork not as 'second best' but as a whole new way of working in a team, with its own specific benefits and drawbacks.

*the name of the client and the company are fictitious in order to protect privacy.

Since then, the team has grown and we have organised and delivered many workshops, most of them in virtual space, helping virtual teams improve their performance, and training leaders of remote teams and trainers in virtual facilitation skills. We are deeply grateful to all our participants for their trust in working with us in this very new field, where many practices are still to be discovered, fine-tuned and researched. With all our groups we have experimented and learned, and this still teaches us every day what works and does not work in virtual communication, leadership and facilitation.

From Jude ...

In her excellent early guide to virtual facilitation (2003) Jennifer Hofmann writes about how being a participant in virtual meetings and learning sessions is one of the best ways to know what works as a virtual trainer and coach, because you still remember your 'first time' participating in cyber space. You remember the way you felt, the fear and the excitement as you started to see how technology and technique could work for you. And later, as a facilitator, you remember how it feels when you get beyond worrying about technological failure and start exploring the possibilities open to you in the virtual meeting or classroom – and you want to connect with that excitement in your participants, because you've been there yourself.

For me, those words are undoubtedly true. While I have been working virtually via phone and later Skype as a coach since 2003, it is only since 2011 that I've experienced the imaginative and explorative playground that virtual platforms can offer in the training, coaching and meeting context.

One of the reasons why it's been such a pleasure to collaborate with Fredrik and our virtual team on this book is because I have indeed 'been there' myself – some four years ago in early 2011 when I was a 'newbie' participant in Nomadic IBP virtual sessions, experiencing every technological problem in the book, and struggling to remain calm whilst quietly panicking about whether my audio would fail me or not.

I still remember those days, and I still experience occasional anxiety and frequent delight every time I run a virtual training session. When I started working as a virtual facilitator, I too saw it as a useful and practical way to expand business and save cost for the client in a severely depressed market. And of course it is all of that, but also something more. Facilitating in the virtual world is an invitation to explore our own creativity, to develop skills we may undervalue, to communicate and engage with people from across the world as if they are sitting next to us, and play with possibilities in ways that really may not be easy or even possible in face to face meetings.

One thing that we are continuing to refine is the harmonious relationship between psychology and technology. For virtual teams to work well together, a certain savvy and ease with communication tools is a necessary prerequisite. Finding some pleasure in trying out new tools, rather than being fearful of them, definitely helps. However, technology is only the starting point. Once a group has decided which tools they like best, and we suggest keeping it fairly simple, the 'psychology' part comes. Here it's about the dynamics of a group of highly diverse people, living in different time zones, often distracted by their local organisations and teams, coming together virtually in order to achieve a common task. Being a member, leader or facilitator of such a group is a new professional field and this book is aimed at helping this target group to be successful in this endeavour.

Since 2012 we have trained many professional facilitators in working virtually with groups and some of them have urged us to share the experience and knowledge we have built over the past half-decade through writing this book. Indeed, the book has been a collective effort by a virtual team, highlighting the advantages of accomplishing a common task, working from our kitchen tables in different countries, while tending to clients, babies, spouses, dogs and other important stakeholders. This brings to mind Jennifer Hofmann's comment that a virtual organisation is like a 'collection of kitchen tables'.

We hope you will enjoy that exhilarating journey of discovery as much as we all have, and share the pleasure of engagement and relationship-building across continents and time zones that 'live' virtual communication offers us all. If in this book we can help to create a spark of excitement in readers new to virtual facilitation, and renewed interest and motivation in those with experience but still unsure of its potential, then we will have achieved what we hoped for in writing this.

Finally, a big word of thanks to our colleagues who have contributed chapters: Sven Cune, Mara Garofalo, Hans Smit and Linda Voorthuis. Also, to Stella McMahon, our designer (www.tambourinedesign.co.uk) and Juliette Vila Sinclair-Spence who have been instrumental in getting this project from a sea of text into a real book. Finally, Kees Smits (www.speedcartooning.nl) who did a wonderful job creating the illustrations.

Happy journeys in virtual space, and please do send us your feedback and questions to the email address below. It is always great to hear about the achievements, challenges, questions and stories of our readers and to respond to these. Please stay in touch via info@nomadicibp.com and our website www.nomadicibp.com.

CONTENTS

THE AUTHORS

Sven Cune

Sven Cune has a MSc. In Organisational Psychology from the University of Amsterdam and used to work as project manager at Nomadic International Business Psychology. Since 2014 he works for Usabilla in the area of optimizing websites. While at university, Sven did research into high performance virtual teams. He also gained a lot of experience in assisting trainers during online training sessions. Sven was born and raised in the Netherlands. Before attending university he lived and studied in Spain and in China where he worked as a trainee consultant and web developer. During this year abroad he developed a passion for cross-cultural communication and he has also worked part time for a helpdesk for visually impaired PC users where he gained a lot of knowledge regarding communication technology.

Fredrik Fogelberg

Fredrik Fogelberg is the owner of Nomadic International Business Psychology, a consultancy specialised in international leadership development, based in the Netherlands. He draws upon almost 30 years' experience in corporate training, cross cultural training, executive coaching and team facilitation. Since the financial crisis in 2008, when many global organisations turned to remote working, he has been building expertise around virtual teams and their leadership. He has published and been an invited speaker on a variety of topics in his field. His special interest is in the group dynamics of intercultural teams, both colocated and geographically dispersed. He is associate faculty of various business schools including the Center for Creative Leadership.

Mara Garofalo

Mara Garofalo is a self-employed coach and facilitator, both face-to-face and virtual, based in Italy. She has developed her practice in the field of leadership, communication and cross-cultural aspects, as well as resilience and ethics, across several continents. She works with different industries and international public institutions. She has incorporated virtual work as a way to deliver internationally and also to collaborate and co-create with colleagues at a distance. Mara is a member of several professional associations and an associate of various organisations, including the Center for Creative Leadership.

Hans Smit

Hans Smit is the owner of Nomadic Meetings based in the Netherlands. Nomadic Meetings provides their clients with the combined services of a meeting platform and producers that offer support to both facilitators and participants before, during and after web trainings and meetings. Prior to this he has gained ample experience in the training and education field working for the largest privately-held Dutch training and education company. Holding degrees in both psychology and information technology, he worked as a consultant in change for several consultancy firms in the Netherlands.

Jude Tavanyar

Jude is an international leadership coach, group facilitator and trainer working since 1987 across Europe, and in US, Asia and Africa. She has worked with global corporations in all industry sectors, training and coaching senior executives to CEO level as an Associate of Centre for Creative Leadership, and others. In her early career Jude was a communications specialist in national public sector organisations, and she has published a book, and numerous articles on leadership, HR, communication and social care issues. A family psychotherapist since 1997, she combines a background in leadership communication with systemic psychology and business experience and knowledge. Jude began her career as a virtual facilitator in 2010, when she trained as a participant on Nomadic's Virtual Facilitation Skills programme. She found she thoroughly enjoyed the approach and now delivers some 50% of her training and coaching over the Internet.

Linda Voorthuis

Linda Voorthuis studied theatre, film and television at the University of Amsterdam, then started her career as video editor and operator in the newsroom of a major Dutch broadcasting company, creating TV news items and operating in live broadcasts. She then moved on to work in the communications department for a globally operating environmental organisation. After a few years of working freelance she became the office manager and virtual training producer at Nomadic IBP.

WHY VIRTUAL FACILITATION?

1

By Fredrik Fogelberg and Jude Tavanyar

Introduction to this book

Imagine this: a group of 8 professionals in leadership development and executive coaching spread out across Europe and Asia want to get together to learn by exchanging experiences. Just a few years ago, they would have had to travel halfway across the globe to meet, and spend a lot of money and time doing so. They would have had the pleasure of eating and drinking together, but the jet lag would also have taken its toll.

Now, through virtual facilitation, they are able to meet once a week over several months and work, learn, play as well as socialise together. Despite the lack of physical contact, the group bonds strongly and its members have real difficulty saying goodbye during the last session.

Of course, such a scenario is no longer imaginary. It is happening already, across the world.

The revolution in the workspace

There is a revolution going on in the world of work. Up until the beginning of the 21st century, work was done in a building where the arrangement was to occupy the same physical space as your co-workers and the boss, come in on time and not leave too early – certainly not before the boss! You were likely to be supervised face to face, and to have numerous conversations with colleagues throughout your working day, whether a round-the-table meeting, a catch-up chat by the coffee machine, or (let's face it, this is where some of the most interesting conversations used to happen) an intriguing piece of 'top secret' gossip shared in the privacy of the washrooms.

Now, for many workers who are not bound by time and place to accomplish their task, work no longer has to be done in one place only. It can be carried out in cafes, libraries, home offices, even while waiting to catch a bus or plane. Whilst this next scenario is far from ideal in our view, we once worked with a colleague running a meeting from his laptop whilst in transit through security at an airport. He had to hold the meeting up for several minutes as his laptop, through which the Internet connection was still running to colleagues scattered across the globe, went through the security scanner and out the other side.

In fact, work now happens anywhere where there is a portable computer, Internet connectivity, and a seat. (Indeed, the seat is optional. Sitting has recently been labelled as 'the new smoking'.) Welcome to the world of remote workers!

If you, like us, regularly work remotely, you will know that our numbers are growing at a terrific rate.

> Between 2005 and 2008, the number of Americans (for example) working remotely increased by 74%, and in the year 2015, 37.2% of the total workforce are predicted to be 'mobile workers' (Global Workplace Analytics, 2014).

By the time the first edition of this book is published in 2015, a staggering 1.3 billion people around the world are working remotely from home or elsewhere (businesswire.com). Are you one of them already?

A survey, conducted by ON in 2012, found that fully 9 in 10 (91%) of HR and training professionals planned to increase the use of virtual training at their companies in 2013, and 1 in 3 (33%) even said they would be increasing use by more than 25% (on24.com, 2012). The survey also found that 64% of people questioned believed that customer/product training is the application best suited for a virtual environment, followed by:

- New Hire On boarding – 62%

- Administrative Topics – 57%

- Sales Training – 48%

- IT Training – 41%.

When asked which characteristics matter most in a virtual trainer, the respondents' top answer was 'Effective user of quizzes, polls and social media' (88%), followed by:

- Facilitation skills – 83%

- Voice inflection – 74%

- Good with technology – 69%

- Topic matter expertise – 60%

- Being Funny – 50%

The case for remote working and 'virtual' communication
Of course, there are some obvious benefits for organisations that are driving what amounts to a transformation in the way work is conducted globally. Four key reasons for this seismic shift from collocated working (working together at the same office base) to virtual working are those of:

- Financial benefit

- Global scope for recruiting talent

- 24 hour availability of personnel

- Increased sophistication and decreased cost of communication technology

Regarding financial benefit, costs are cut in three ways by organisations with remote workers. Firstly, because the business no longer needs to supply as much office space to its employees (with all the additional costs that buildings carry), and secondly, because travel costs to meetings are cut to a minimum, including the cost of time 'away from desk' for each travelling employee. Thirdly, remote working offers business the opportunity to outsource work to countries with lower labour costs.

As far as recruiting talent is concerned, talent management has itself been a key challenge for businesses of all kinds for some years. Previously the possibilities of finding and retaining talented staff were significantly limited by geographical constraints, but not anymore.

Remote working provides the option of selecting team members from a range of locations – we are talking continents, in some cases – based on their competence, rather than relying on personnel who happen to be based in the area in which the business operates.

The third – and immeasurable – benefit to business is the possibility that all organisations have these days, through remote working, to achieve a 24 hour workplace. When team members are spread across time zones, while those in one part of the world may be asleep, others elsewhere are hard at work, providing round-the-clock continuity of effort.

Fourthly, the technology that makes it possible for us to speak, see, hear each other across distance is likely to become ever more sophisticated and affordable, so that the business case for achieving close connections and productive, high-functioning relationships without being in the same room as our colleagues becomes increasingly compelling.

Just a few years ago, all these changes would have been unthinkable. But, in less than a few years from now, the idea of going to the same workplace as your colleagues by car or public transport and sharing office space with them is likely to seem a ludicrously outmoded approach to the world of work. We are more likely to be commuting via robotic systems.

In the final chapter of this book we take a look in more depth at some of the technological and other trends which may shape our working lives in years to come, knowing that even at the time of writing we may be out-of-date in our predictions in the rapidly-changing world we find ourselves in.

The other side of the coin

So where is the 'but' in these arguments? Can remote working really offer exactly the same benefits to business as our well-established, co-located approach via good, old-fashioned, in-the-same-place presence?

'Aha' (you may be saying) 'Of course not! There are some things about face to face contact that technology cannot replace!' And of course, you are right.

In some cultures, a trusted business relationship is built upon physical contact, smell, and (even) taste of our working partners and colleagues. Although the world of work is changing, we are arguably still some way off being able to sniff our clients' after-shave, deliver a firm handshake, eat a meal together, or apply three kisses to our colleagues via Internet technology. We explore the exciting challenge of being effective as a virtual communicator with culturally diverse groups of participants in *Chapter Eight*.

Also, research shows that remote working does not fit all individuals. Depending on their personality and character traits, people respond differently to its advantages and downsides (Meulen van der, 2014).

But who knows what is around the corner? In our final chapter we talk about current trends and future possibilities, the positive and the potentially negative alike. One challenge in writing a chapter like this is that, necessarily, we gauge the future through the lens of past experience and present realities. And of course that lens presents a rather limited vision. Given that already today – as this chapter discusses – technological trends are shaping our lives in ways we would never have thought possible just a very few years ago, perhaps it is time to assume that what we consider technologically impossible now may – almost in the blink of an eye – shortly become a reality. For, in the brave new world of virtual communication, technology seems increasingly able to take even the most feverish figments of our imagination and bring them to electronic life.

However, whether or not technological advancement represents a glorious plaything, the affirmation of our capacity as human beings to communicate in ever more imaginative ways, or a kind of uncontrollable, all-powerful Frankenstein's monster – the breath-taking spiral of technological advancement is, here to stay, whether we like it or not.

An overview of this book

In **Chapter Two** of this book, we invite you to overcome any reluctance you may have to explore some of the key technologies available in virtual communication. We do not wish here to dazzle you with the brilliance of what is available, or to leave you feeling 'under-skilled' from a technological point of view. In fact, the opposite – this chapter is a down-to-earth practical overview of available technologies, and offers some useful pointers in helping you select the most appropriate platform for your purposes as a virtual communicator. It also provides a basic 'how to' guide to some of the most important and useful technological features that are easily accessible, even to those with a beginner's interest and a limited budget.

Apart from assisting you in becoming more confident and competent with technology, we want to get beyond the idea in this book that 'technology is king'. It may be, but only if we let it rule us. Dealing smoothly and competently with an unpredictable software platform is a bit like dealing with a moody but often brilliant boss. You need strategies to manage a tricky boss, just as you need them to prevent and manage technology 'glitches'. We provide these, and while we hope you may not need them, they're there if you do.

In any case, managing technology does not need to be a lonely task, and practice makes perfect. In **Chapter Three** of this book, we look at one of the greatest, behind-the-scenes supports any budding or experienced virtual facilitator could hope for – the **producer**. The producer is the technological support person for you, the facilitator, whatever virtual event or meeting you are leading. S/he takes care of 'all things technological' and assists participants with any challenges they may face in joining, and attending your virtual event. Believe us, your producer is worth his or her weight in gold. We have a producer whose commitment to her role is so significant that she was prepared to get out of bed at 3 am and provide last-minute technological support for an important US client training one dark winter's night in central Europe. The producer booked for the role had gotten the days mixed up because of the time zone differences.

We can hardly do justice to the value of the producer's role without gushing foolishly. So let us gush: this person is **invaluable** not only during the session/s you are running, but before and after, providing assistance with all matters technical, and providing calm, capable, unflappable back-up so that any kind of virtual 'event' or meeting can continue even when there are problems 'back-stage'. Teamwork and effective communication between producer and facilitator is, as you might imagine, therefore very important, and we cover it in detail in this chapter.

One key reason for writing this book is because many people have become (like us) bored with the monologue-style 'passive presentation' format of many forms of 'live' synchronous meetings over the Internet – the 'standard' webinar being one of the best known. Even the word webinar itself, suggesting a web lecture of some kind where the tutor's voice takes precedence, tends to have a somewhat dispiriting effect upon the listener.

A new approach to virtual communication and learning is, we believe, long overdue. In our **Chapter Four on session design in virtual space** we link current learning theories with the design of virtual communication sessions, exploring how to devise and design engaging and exciting virtual learning meetings and programmes that dovetail with a variety of learners' needs. Knowing participants' learning styles, cultural differences, personality preferences, and so forth, will have an important effect in shaping the design decisions of your coaching, training and consulting meeting activities.

This chapter also looks at how people absorb and 'process' information in virtual space differently to the way they do in a face to face setting. We discuss the concept of 'virtual closeness', and of managing group dynamics in virtual space; we also offer practical guidance on influencing such challenges. Finally, we present some examples and case studies of powerful and effective programme design; and the 'design pitfalls' to avoid.

And of course powerful virtual communication is not just about using sophisticated software platforms, or expert design strategies – but about applying psychology in practice. And if 'psychology' sounds like quite a big word to use in this context – we mean the ideas, working principles, strategies and behaviours on your side of the screen that will keep people engaged with you across the globe.

The ways of keeping that much-needed engagement from our colleagues or clients may vary enormously between individuals, and the topic of how to achieve that in your own style when working virtually is, again, one that has been given scant attention until now.

In **Chapter Five** of this book we explore the elements that contribute to virtual facilitation 'style' – in other words, the aspects of virtual communication that may determine how YOU uniquely come across to others, and the impact you make when communicating across distance. Apart from discussing in more depth the required tasks, skills and role of a facilitator, whether you are a trainer, coach or manager running meetings – we share current theories and our own model for developing your facilitation style in virtual space. This chapter includes some sound practical tips for coming across in the way that brings out your 'best self' as a virtual facilitator, and will keep your participants and meeting attendees coming back for more.

This book is not just about learning events, however. In **Chapter Six** we focus on the topic of **running meetings virtually**. We look at why some virtual meetings don't achieve their objectives, why some people literally dread both running, and attending, them – and how to change this. We highlight behaviours and practices for the meeting Chairperson through which we aim to turn your dislike (if such it is) of virtual meetings into interest, even enthusiasm – as both virtual meeting Chair and attendee.

As stated above, one way to overcome technological unpredictability is to learn some basic practical techniques and spend time getting a hands-on grasp of any virtual communication platform, in order to acquire competence and (just as importantly) confidence in your skills. Another way to deal with technological 'cold feet' is by having (human) back-up.

While the ideas and practical tips we offer in the book are relevant whatever kind of virtual meeting you are running, we consider it important to dedicate **Chapter Six** to virtual meetings alone. This is partly because meetings over distance are such a familiar part of everyday life now that they are almost taken for granted, even though they are so often run with less than full engagement, attention and effectiveness. And this ineffectiveness clearly has a significant cost in terms of wasted employee time and lowered performance.

In **Chapter Seven** we explore **how to work with different kinds of audiences** in cyber space, and in different contexts. While it is a glaringly obvious truth to say that no two clients or organisations are the same, we believe that it is helpful to look at some audience profiles and 'types', whether you work with training groups, executive coaching clients, teams, senior managers, and/or your own colleagues. The 'group from hell' – excuse the expression – will also be described. Perhaps you already have some experience of working with this group – and what to do as a facilitator when you meet it!

Chapter Eight tackles **virtual facilitation with diverse cultural audiences**, a topic we believe to be very much overlooked when communicating virtually. Drawing on (between us) well over 60 years of experience in working cross-culturally, and as members of a culturally diverse remote team ourselves, we offer here a valuable exploration of the key differences between national cultures that may impact upon virtual sessions, and the theories upon which these are based. Most importantly, we also show how to work with these and turn them into an advantage, backed with plenty of examples, models, guidance and practical activities for working effectively with these stimulating but sometimes challenging groups.

In virtual space the shortcut some trainers may feel tempted to take of not adjusting content and agenda to a specific client's needs will show up all the more powerfully. There is so much else to distract the virtual learner or meeting attendee from your presentation or activity – emails, phone calls, a coffee or toilet break, even falling asleep – that customisation of content to client's needs to minimize boredom and distraction has never been more essential.

The last two chapters of this book are somewhat broader in scope. In **Chapter Nine**, we look at the **consultant's role and useful strategies in helping organisations get ready for culture change**, if they are wishing to shift to a 'virtual communication approach' to a greater or lesser extent. This chapter argues that, when introducing the possibilities of virtual communication via (for example) online 'live' meetings into an organisation, it is essential to take the wider context of the organisation's culture – beliefs, values, challenges, prejudices, achievements, history – into account and work with what already 'is'.

Change may be a constant in today's world but it does not always happen overnight, with a single workshop or training, even with the most passionate advocacy from a virtual communications expert, or following a sensationally successful virtual training programme.

This chapter addresses some of the factors to take into consideration when discussing an assignment for virtual facilitation with your (organisational) client. It should help your client benefit from the many advantages offered by virtual contact, and avoid the disadvantages of time-wasting, expense, frustrations and employee demotivation if the requested changes are rushed through, or introduced without care and consideration at all levels.

In **Chapter Ten**, the final one in this book, we venture playfully into the **future** and predict what virtual learning and meeting may look like in the next ten years or so. We explore how current trends may translate into products and services in the decade to come, if (and there is no reason to doubt this) the rate of technological advancement continues at its existing breath-taking pace. We also invite you to consider how these developments may affect you, as a communicator across distance.

This book is, above all, a practical guide packed with ideas, activities, resources, tips and anecdotes. In putting it together, we trawled a broad range of sources; our own combined experience as a remote team of trainers, coaches and consultants, and the stories and feedback of our clients and students over the years are not least among them.

 Within each chapter, you will find practical tips and actions that relate to the theme of the chapter. These are shown with a 'spanner symbol' for easy recognition.

We end with **Resources**, offering you a large number of materials to help you prepare, design and deliver effective virtual events of all kinds, and Resources that we hope you will find useful in developing your virtual communication work.

Finally, whether you decide to explore the many possibilities and tools that virtual communication provides you with, or stick to a single, tried-and-tested approach, is entirely up to you. We have written this book for anyone at any level of professional life who seeks to use virtual communication in groups more powerfully and effectively, whether as trainers, coaches, consultants, leaders and/or team members spread across multiple locations.

We owe much to the generous contributions of the remote learning community within which we work – past and current students, clients, colleagues alike, and thank them for their generosity in sharing their ideas and insights for our book. The words of Elsa, a recent participant on one of our virtual training programmes, strike us particularly now, in writing this.

'When I first joined your training programme, I was struck by how free-flowing, spontaneous, playful – even messy – it seemed at times' said Elsa. 'You had a structure but you dropped it at times when participants wanted to have time to discuss and explore something freely. This is not the approach we notice in the usual 'webinar' setting. It's suggesting a massive shift of mindset, a transformation in the way we think about virtual learning and communication.'

The 'shift of mind-set' Else speaks of, from the 'presentational webinar' approach – with its one-way delivery to large groups of muted attendees – is already underway. However while people continue to regard virtual communication as a kind of 'second best' to its face to face equivalent, a way of making contact necessitated by distance and budget constraints, we think that they are missing the point.

Not just translation, but innovation?
In this book, we argue that virtual communication is far more than the humble replacement of physical presence, a way of 'translating' face to face activities into the virtual realm. Indeed, we seek to present it as a deeply exciting and engaging way for human beings to interact, a different form of communicating altogether, with its own principles and practices, its own innovative appeal and advantages.

If you were participating in one of our meetings, training or coaching sessions, you would notice frequent interruption, laughter, visual stimuli to trigger discussion via slide or whiteboard, doodling as well as writing, gossip, rapid 'chat' exchanges, team games and activities, and a generally convivial atmosphere where ideas are shared and debated freely.

We believe it is this combination of playful elements and a (sometimes) unpredictable agenda that make virtual communication such a highly valuable means of sharing knowledge and ideas and of creating and deepening relationships between individuals and teams. We also believe the kind of 'messy' spontaneity that Elsa refers to, the intentional informality and interactivity of approach, the friendly, sociable atmosphere you might find by the coffee machine in any face to face training event are key elements of the departure from 'one way' monologue-style webinar presentations in the virtual world.

We trust that this is an inspiring and provocative message that will stimulate people who may have avoided meeting virtually until now, fearing that it might be too formal, or disengaging, or even 'clinical', lacking the 'human connection' that brings face to face meetings to life. We really hope that this book will encourage facilitators with all levels of experience to extend their skills further, to try out new ideas and activities, and build confidence in the enormous potential that this form of communication offers.

References

1) Globalworkplaceanalytics.com 2014
2) Businesswire.com 2014
3) Gigaom.com 2011
4) On24.com, 2014
5) Meulen, van der Nick, (2014). Erasmus @work Research briefing # 6. RSM Erasmus University, de staat van het nieuwe werken.

VIRTUAL COMMUNICATION TECHNOLOGY

2

By Sven Cune and Jude Tavanyar

'Technology gives us power, but it does not and cannot tell us how to use that power. Thanks to technology, we can instantly communicate across the world, but it still doesn't help us know what to say.'
Jonathan Sacks

Introduction – Feel the Fear and Do It Anyway?

If there is one topic which strikes fear into the heart of any trainer or public speaker, whether presenting face to face or virtually, it is technological failure. Anyone who has been embarrassed in front of their audience or team by the vagaries and whims of technology – the errant slide deck that refuses to upload to screen, the soundless video, the failing microphone – all you people will know exactly why we have dedicated an entire chapter to mastering technology in a book about virtual communication.

As many of us see it, there is only one rule to pay attention to when using technology to communicate: If it can go wrong, it will. Which is, without a doubt, a key reason why so many people refuse to 'go virtual' and use the multiple opportunities that synchronous online communication can offer us.

And yet, there is little evidence that technological failure is either as frequent or, even when it occurs, as disastrous as we might imagine. It is quite likely that, just as a newspaper reporting only 'good news' would be of little interest to many, the reason why technological failure is such a commonplace fear is because the many, many occasions when technology serves us smoothly and without error tend to go unnoticed. Just like a 'good news' newspaper, they are too boring to merit our attention, perhaps.

Apart from reassuring the technophobe or even the mildly technology-resistant, there are two other good reasons for including this chapter. One is that technology is, of course, here to stay, astonishingly diverse and also increasingly versatile. Virtual meetings, online training and coaching sessions, webinars, virtual events of all kinds are all made possible by the wonders of technological wizardry, the broad and varied spectrum of 'platforms' and channels that allow us to make contact with each other across vast distances.

And of course the level of sophistication of these possibilities varies from   say – simple text messaging at one end of the scale to advanced video conferencing at the other, with a very great deal in between. Not knowing how to access and use the technologies available at low cost via the Internet for online communication is already a limitation and increasingly will become a serious drawback for the successful trainer, facilitator, manager or coach in today's global marketplace.

So, in this chapter we will discuss how to:

- familiarise yourself with virtual communication technology

- prevent and deal with technology-related problems when meeting virtually

- learn practical and universally-applicable guidelines to help you decide when to use which technology

- explore how to select a technology provider/supplier.

There is one extremely important aspect of technological proficiency which we do not cover here, but in a separate chapter as it merits some detailed focus. In **Chapter Three**, we explore the role and importance of that most valuable of all assets – the technical producer.

Knowing what technology to use when, and how to use it is of course key in virtual facilitation. But we offer this chapter with two provisos. First of all, virtual communication technology is such a rapidly-growing area that it is likely that some of the points made below may be out of date by the time you read them, even if the main messages of the chapter are not.

And secondly do not be deceived into thinking that if you are a technological expert, you have all the skills you need to lead meetings of all kinds and generally communicate well virtually. Without a large helping of insight, understanding, a willingness to engage with feedback and to vary one's style to suit a broad range of participants' needs, technological courage may very well take you off the starting blocks but it will most definitely not get you across the finishing line.

> *'Technology is just a tool. In terms of getting (people) working together and motivating them, the teacher is the most important.'*
> **Bill Gates**

Learning to use technology

As we often say in our virtual training sessions: the technological information learned in our dedicated module on this topic applies to all web meeting platforms. Learning to facilitate virtually is therefore a bit like learning to drive a car. At first you are nervously looking for the right gear and you feel you have to divide your attention over a hundred things at the same time; but then, after a little more practice, everything starts to go smoothly and you find you can shift your focus from driving the car to what is going on around you. What at first felt like an effort of concentration becomes easy and natural, almost unconscious.

Exactly the same goes for virtual facilitation. As soon as you know your way around the platform, you can direct your attention towards what is most important – your training participants. At this stage, the technology becomes no more than a medium for communication. Requiring no great mental focus from the facilitator at this point, using the technology rapidly becomes a natural, almost unthinking action. It just doesn't play a big role anymore.

Prevention is Better than Cure – Tips for Managing Minor Technical Challenges
The reality is that even the most experienced facilitator delivering an online session together with a very experienced producer can, and quite often does, get into trouble. The good news is that it is possible to prepare even for these scenarios, and that preparation is usually fairly straightforward. Dealing smoothly with potential derailing factors can make all the difference between success and catastrophe in virtual space, whatever the scale of the problem.

PRACTICAL GUIDELINES

Here are some practical guidelines to help you cope with some of the most common technological challenges.

- **Use a 'wired' Internet connection:** Although a wireless connection can be very fast and stable, it will always be less so then a wired internet connection. Other devices and Wi-Fi networks around your computer and router will scramble your wireless connection, slowing it down and making it less reliable. A good rule to keep in mind when it comes to disaster prevention is to eliminate as many pitfalls as possible. A wireless connection is one of them.

- **Technology check:** You can choose to perform an individual technology check with each participant joining a session. This means that you connect with each participant individually, and set up a one-to-one session in advance of the main meeting to see if the participant can connect to the web meeting platform.

  We have learned from experience that participants joining virtual meetings from company networks sometimes have limited access to external software, including access to web meeting platforms, so this early check is very well worthwhile to ensure smooth access to the platform. Keep in mind of course that the participant needs to connect to the technology check session from the same computer as the one he or she will use during the actual training sessions.

  Performing technical checks can be quite time-consuming, especially if you work with large audiences. However it is worth every second you spend on it, in terms of participants being able to join the session smoothly, and have the best audio connections from the start.

  If we are working with a group of people based at the same office site, we may choose to limit ourselves to running a technical check with a minimum of one participant from that office location. It's very likely that if one person can join from a specific company network, the same goes for others joining from the same network.

- **Send a link to a 'test' virtual meeting room:** There is always the option to send participants beforehand a link to an asynchronous technical check (see 2.1 in the **Resources** section at the back of this book – **Default Invitation**). Many platforms have test meeting rooms open constantly in this way, so that participants can join at a time that suits them. Be aware, of course, that while this option is obviously less time-consuming, there is no guarantee that participants will actually perform this asynchronous 'tech check'.

- **Include a 'kick off'/initial 'try out' session in your programme or meeting design.** In this way, you build in an informal event during which participants can get used to the technology of the virtual classroom. During the 'Kick-off' session there is typically less attention spent on content, and far more on technology so that participants can explore and address technological issues – simply finding their way around the platform, the interactive and feedback tools, for example – before you seek to begin delivering the specific content of the programme or event itself.

  And if this sounds at first like an optional 'add-on' to your programme, it isn't. Kick-off or 'try out' sessions are highly advisable. You will eventually gain considerable time and limit frustrations with technology if you do this. Conversely, trying to jump straight into 'training content' in the first ten minutes of any session without allowing the participants time to get comfortable with technical aspects of the platform will prevent you from facilitating effectively, and participants from learning much. A kick-off session is an essential investment with guaranteed payback later in the programme.

While these tips to help you prepare are very useful in preventing the most common (and avoidable) technical challenges, there will still be times when you are faced with more serious difficulties that potentially can derail your online session. These range from participants who do not follow instructions properly and end up in the wrong meeting (yes – it happens!), to a complete power cut, leaving the facilitator without a producer in front of a group of 20 participants.

Again, knowing and anticipating some of these disaster scenarios helps, because it is possible in some cases to have a 'Plan B' when they occur.

Disaster Management and Recovery

'Disaster' is a big word. However, we're using it broadly here to include a range of scenarios that are likely to occur at some point in your career as a virtual facilitator. Sadly, even with the best prevention strategy, it is just not possible to control all the external factors that affect the reliability of your online sessions.

Here are some typical 'disaster scenarios':

- Participant cannot connect to the platform

- Wrong link to session is sent out to participants

- Facilitator's computer stops working

- Internet connection drops

- A power cut affects a number of participants.

If the case of any of the above scenarios, there are two things to do. The first, of course, is not to panic. The second is to ask yourself a key question.

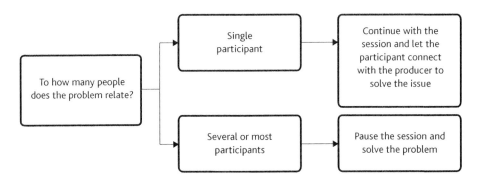

Does the problem affect only one or two participants? Or does it affect more people? Whenever the issue applies only to one participant, let the producer take care of it while you continue with the session. It is very likely that the producer is busy connecting to participants constantly throughout a session in any case, to fix small audio 'glitches', for example.

If the issue **does** affect several people or the whole group, there is really no point in continuing with the session, you will need to stop facilitating and solve the issue at hand.

How to do that? Here are some recovery tips.

RECOVERY TIPS

- **Keep the session details handy.** If you get disconnected for whatever reason from a session you will be able to reconnect swiftly if you have the login details written down somewhere. If the platform that you are using offers both VOIP and telephone as dial-in options, make sure that you know how to connect through both options. You will then be able to switch quickly and easily if one of the options fails to work.

- **Participant list and email addresses must also be kept close at hand.** Both the producer and the facilitator should have immediate access to a participant list that contains at least the email addresses of all participants. If somehow a session is interrupted and a new session needs to be launched on the fly, the new joining instructions will need to be communicated quickly to all participants.

- **Second computer set up.** If you often deliver virtual sessions, it is worthwhile to invest in a second computer and have it ready at hand. Then you have a rapid fall-back option if your 'usual' computer for delivery crashes for any reason.

- **Second meeting platform.** Access to technology becomes easier and cheaper all the time, and thus the average computer user has often one or more communicators installed, like Skype or Lync. This means that if you are in a virtual meeting and technology fails, you can find another common technology and switch to that.

- **Second producer.** This may now start to sound a little far-fetched, but we have learned the hard way that it is very handy to have a producer on standby who can jump in if the actual producer is unable to join at the last minute. And yes, that has happened more than once over the years, and doubtless will happen again! So it is vital to keep all information related to a virtual session stored in one common place, otherwise the standby producer will not be able to step in and launch the session, without access to the session details.

Unfortunately not all disasters listed here can be prevented by applying these guidelines. If you experience a power cut or the internet fails to work, this is, of course, out of your control. At moments like these, again, a producer will prove to be invaluable. When you as a facilitator are disconnected from the session, the producer can inform the participants about the situation and stall if necessary. This will give you time to find a solution and reconnect.

If by now you are starting to feel that virtual facilitation is just one long series of technical nightmares – disasters which cannot be predicted or circumvented but simply 'managed' as well as possible – you are right and wrong at the same time. While it certainly is the case that the kind of disasters we list here do occur, they are by no means common and you will probably run numerous sessions without any insurmountable challenges – for the entire period of your session.

That said, having a Plan B is always a good idea. Not only because it may help you to feel comfortable and relaxed as a facilitator if you know what to do when something – on whatever scale –goes wrong, but also because it will really help your participants if you can keep them engaged when technical challenges occur.

Discussing and negotiating such challenges in advance – who will do what in certain circumstances – is partly down to the relationship you build with your producer/s and taking time for a clear exploration of disaster prevention and recovery. What facilitators and producers expect from each other varies significantly, even though the roles are quite different, and it is very important to be clear about your combined approach for managing technological setbacks of every kind.

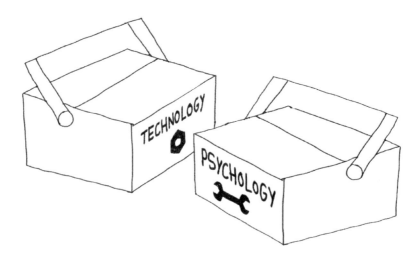

Choosing a technology

One of the technical challenges facing a virtual facilitator communicator, is actually choosing the most appropriate technological platform for their needs in the first place – especially as the range of technologies available increases so rapidly that it's almost impossible to stay entirely up to date.

However, there is some good news. There are some easy pointers (based on available research) to help you decide which technology to use in any given situation, whether you are selecting a full-scale platform for training delivery to which you need to make a significant financial commitment (see Choosing a Provider below), or selecting from a range of free channels for a quick communication with a colleague.

Each technology has its own strengths and weaknesses, depending on the features it has. To decide which technology and features you need, you need to begin by defining the task you seek to accomplish.

Matching the technology to the task

In this next section, we go into quite a lot of detail on this point about matching task to technology. Some readers may feel that it holds no great surprises, since the rules are clear and easy to understand. Others may be surprised to look at what research tells us about matching task and communication technology.

Whatever your reactions, we cannot emphasise strongly enough the importance of getting right this match of technology to task. Why? Because, year after year, email traffic increases and executives the world over continue to misunderstand each other simply because they view the written word as a simple, rapid means to convey almost any message, no matter how sensitive or complex. In doing so, they ignore the reality that the apparent speed and convenience of sending an email for every kind of communication in the short-term may mean time-consuming confusion in the longer-term. Without visual contact and a synchronous conversation, undiscussed assumptions and misinterpretations on the kind of topics that are too delicate or complex for written communication alone will continue to proliferate.

Using email inappropriately is a fairly well-known topic. But it is also astonishing how, to take another example, poorly run video-conferences continue to frustrate and irritate executives the world over. Points of detail that could be shared swiftly and without discussion – via email or other written exchange may, in a badly chaired meeting without a clear agenda, provoke endless debate and diversionary conversation – to no real effect or outcome.

Using the 'Task and Technology' Matrix

The relationship between task and technology has been researched by Eggen (2013), and involved interviews with virtual workers from different backgrounds and cultures globally.

In the diagram below we have transposed some of the results of this research, showing you how certain technologies perform against certain kinds of tasks.

In general, it is possible to allocate most professional tasks into three categories:

- **Routine tasks.** These are straightforward tasks that you may complete regularly, and which may simply involve a one-way exchange of information to another person or people. This kind of task does not involve discussion, exploration or dialogue. One example might be informing a colleague about a meeting time which has already been decided.

- **Non Routine tasks.** These are more complex tasks that require some thinking and which are not part of your daily 'routine'. They may involve discussion and debate, sharing views and selecting ideas. One example might be collaborating with colleagues to discuss and design a new training programme or product launch.

- **Building and Maintaining Relationships.** These are tasks which might include talking with others to improve relationships in conflictual situations, to understand colleagues who you do not know well, or to build a new team. One example might be having a sociable conversation with a new team member to help him or her feel welcome and to get to know the person better.

Each of these tasks or activities clearly makes different demands from technology. Eggen's research, as set out in the model below, shows these three categories of task slightly differently, as follows:

- The category of 'Routine tasks' is renamed as 'Producing documents'

- The category 'Non-Routine Tasks' is divided into three activities: 'Producing documents', 'Explaining/having Difficult Conversations' and 'Brainstorming and Discussing'

- The category of Building Relationships is shown as a third and distinct category.

We include the Task-Technology Matrix here as a clear and visual means to address some of those tricky questions of technology choice for the less experienced virtual communicator.

	Exchanging information	Producing documents	Explaining/ having difficult conversations	Brainstormin and discussing	Building relationships
Email	:)	:)	:(	:(	:|
Text message	:)	:(	:(	:(	:)
Chat	:)	:|	:|	:|	:)
Phone	:)	:(	:|	:)	:)
Phone conference	:(	:(	:|	:|	:|
Video conference	:(	:|	:)	:)	:)
Video conference 2.0 (Halo/Telepresence)	:(	:)	:)	:)	:)
Web meeting platform	:(	:)	:)	:)	:)

How to use the information shown here? As the 'Task-Technology Matrix' suggests, the first point is to decide before you start what kind of 'task' or activity this is – routine, non-routine, or related to building relationships.

Then you need to consider what any particular technology offers you. Rather surprisingly, available research tells us that, even in these days of increasing technological sophistication and diversity, there are really still only **three aspects** of technological function that matter here. They are:

- The technology's ability to provide 'informational richness'
- The technology's ability to offer 'social presence'
- Whether the technology is effective for achieving 'asynchronous' or 'synchronous' communication.

What do these terms mean?

Firstly, **'informational richness'**. This refers to the degree of information that the technology can convey, quickly and simply. Taking email again as an example, one can easily imagine that it offers considerable 'informational richness', allowing users the option to share plenty of information via attached documents and in the body of the email itself.

Secondly, **'social presence'**. This describes the amount of social interaction a technology provides. For example, a Skype call with the webcam switched on provides quite high social presence – participants can see each other and communicate in 'real time', hearing each other's voices and seeing facial and body moments 'live', exactly when they happen. Platforms like Skype or WebEx can be, as users will know, surprisingly effective in giving the impression of 'closeness' and 'presence' – even though those involved may be thousands of miles apart.

Thirdly, the terms 'asynchronous' and 'synchronous' relate, of course, to whether or not the technology allows people the possibility to communicate and interact **at the same moment** – synchronously – regardless of the time zone they are in, or 'asynchronously', when the **communication is made at a particular time, but may not be seen, received and responded to by the recipient until some time later.** (Email is of course one example of asynchronous communication – although sometimes it is sent by one person and seen by another only seconds later, this is not necessarily the case.)

One point to make about this distinction is that asynchronous communication technologies like email makes dialogue – where an exchange of ideas is required, for example – more tricky because of the time delay between message and response that can be involved, and the possibility of misinterpreting a written message without being able to verify it on the spot. On the other hand, synchronous technology – like a video-conference – allows simultaneous discussion and exchange with plenty of possibility to explore ideas and ensure understanding of key messages and perspectives. This, as we mentioned earlier, does not make it a simple and rapid way to ensure a swift sharing of information, where no exchange is needed, like email.

Choosing a provider

So now you are (hopefully) full of practical tips and suggestions about technology, and want to start facilitating sessions. Great! You have come to the moment where you have to decide which provider you will actually use for this delivery.

Looking at the Task vs. Technology Matrix set out above, we can see that for training purposes it makes most sense to find a platform that offers both informational richness and social presence. Facilitating training corresponds broadly with the category of 'Brainstorming and Discussing' on the Task vs. Technology Matrix – in which case, a web meeting platform would be the most suitable option.

However, from this point your choice becomes a little more complicated. In the 'subcategory' of technologies listed under 'Web Meeting Platforms', there is an endless number of possibilities. Some of the best-known names in this industry are:

> WebEx by Cisco,
> GoTo series by Citrix (GoToMeeting/webinar/training)
> Adobe Connect
> Microsoft Lync.

To make life just a little more complicated, there are further options within each platform option. All these suppliers offer different versions of their platform; for example a version for meetings, webinars with large audiences and training sessions.

If you are now wilting slightly, it helps to realise that, as communication technologies continue to develop and become more sophisticated, the overlap in functions and features between technologies becomes very considerable. Take Skype, for example. Starting as a tool allowing voice presence over the Internet (VOIP), then later on enabling video calls also, it now offers screen sharing as well. This means that Skype offers basically the same features as the most basic versions of web meeting platforms like WebEx Meeting Center and GoToMeeting.

Confusing, isn't it? It's not surprising that in many cases navigating your way around available technologies can be a bewildering and frustrating process. If you are finding that it is rather difficult to choose the provider that's right for you – or think that you may come up against that problem in the future – here are a few steps below that can make this process a little easier.

Steps to help you choose your Technology Platform for Virtual Facilitation

- Establish your technology need, using the Task vs. Technology Matrix

- Once you know which type of technology you will use, research the Internet and compare platforms* according to the criteria which meet your needs

- Request trial versions for several platforms (ask for free extended trials, this is increasingly possible and negotiable with eager salespeople)

- Set up test meetings or pilot training sessions with colleagues or friends. This is the only way you can experience the level of 'user-friendliness' of the various platforms.

* When writing this book, we considered giving an overview of the different platforms and their functions. However, technology moves on rapidly, far more quickly than book publication timelines. In order to stay abreast of the numerous possibilities on offer, please visit supplier websites and get the relevant information direct, and feel free to experiment and practice as much as you can before making any kind of choice.

Enlist the help of your friendly 'company nerd'

There's one in almost every company. If you get lost in the forest of technologies and providers, simply ask for help from the 'company nerd'. Almost everyone has somebody in their direct surroundings, a colleague or a friend, who is technology-savvy, if not you yourself. Preferably this should be someone from within your own company, who really enjoys experimenting with new software and communication technologies.

Your friendly company 'nerd' can also, apart from supporting you through the sea of information that faces you once you look into technological possibilities, act as advocate for a new approach at a later stage, pushing its adaptation with those who hold the purse-strings.

The 'nerd' is therefore an absolutely vital resource – support, advocate, and source of general help, the 'go-to guy or girl' when other users have questions or problems with technology. His or her advice and support can save you valuable time (and money) when exploring appropriate technology for your needs.

And once you have the technology in place, you will want to think about designing meetings, training and coaching sessions for maximum engagement, enjoyment and impact. And that is what we talk about in our next chapter.

References

1) Drew, C. K. W., Weingart, L. R., (2003) Task Versus Relationship Conflict, Team Performance, and Team Member Satisfaction: A Meta-Analysis.

2) Duarte, D. L., Snyder, N. T., (2006)Mastering Virtual Teams: Strategies, Tools, and Techniques That Succeed.

3) Eggen, A. H. M., (2013) The Relationship between Task, Culture and Communication Technology in Virtual Collaboration.

AN EXTRA PAIR OF HANDS IN CYBER SPACE:

The Producer Role

By Linda Voorthuis

3

Wanted: *High-energy all-round technical wizard with extraordinary stress management skills, high level emotional intelligence, unfailing sense of humour, ability to multi-task at all times, speak several languages, comfort distressed facilitators and manage frustrated participants and still sound calm and relaxed. Could this be you?*

I am a successful producer working with globally-spread groups in virtual training and coaching programmes since 2010. During that time, I've been asked frequently what a producer is and why it's useful to have one.

What is a producer ?

The quick answer is this: the person who deals with the technical aspects of the virtual event – whatever it may be – working in the background to ensure the virtual session runs smoothly. The producer is really the facilitator's 'right hand' man or woman, not just during the session, but before and after it as well.

On the other hand, there could be many answers to the question, because although there are certainly key tasks that most facilitators would expect a producer to fulfil, the scope of the role varies according to:

- the facilitator's approach
- the kind of session that is being run
- and specific client needs.

This chapter will explore the producer role, and range of tasks, in more depth. But first, here's a colleague's anecdote from four years ago – her first experience of a webinar – that highlights what a producer can do to help the facilitator, especially in a large group webinar setting.

'There were apparently more than 200 people joining this webinar, which was being run on effective communication skills. However, it seemed apparent within just a few minutes that the presenter was inexperienced. He pointed out almost at once that, while most attendees were joining from Europe, he was joining the webinar from the US at 5 am local time, and his voice sounded drained of energy and flat. It was quite hard to listen to him solidly for an hour, and as the topic was about communication, this was off-putting.

Then things started to go wrong. In the middle of talking about some slides, a mobile phone rang, quite loudly. The presenter's, of course– everyone else was muted for the entire presentation. We heard quite noisy fumbling in a briefcase and the man said briskly: 'That's my phone. Sorry about that.' He'd forgotten to switch it off or turn the volume down.

A little later, there was a knock at the door. The presenter said, quite audibly, 'I'm running a webinar session in here! I don't want the room cleaned!' And the door shut again. So he was working from a hotel room and had forgotten to notify staff. We heard some frustrated sighing and the session went on ... and on. It was rather boring – probably the worst webinar I have ever attended, and all those mistakes were easy to avoid.'

We all have our 'off days' as facilitators, although the above anecdote highlights some pretty basic errors which a more experienced person would have avoided. However, if this unfortunate facilitator had used a producer, what could have been different? The short answer is – everything.

A producer could have advised the facilitator to arrange the meeting at a convenient time for him, as well as the attendees (ie not first thing in the morning, when your voice has barely 'warmed up'). A producer could have intervened to keep the session going while the presenter had to go 'offline' to quietly turn off his phone. Finally, a producer could have taken over again when the external interruption by the cleaner occurred (or reminded the facilitator beforehand to put a sign on the bedroom door letting people know not to disturb him).

Most importantly perhaps, a producer could have contributed in this session vocally, by adding comments at times – this is far more interesting for attendees than hearing the same voice (especially when it's a dull, tired one) for the entire session.

In fact, the role of the producer seems to have developed over time, in the same way as virtual events themselves have moved from being (initially, at least) rather passive, monologue-style affairs with muted participants and a single presenter, to more interactive, dialogue-led exchanges, often with a strongly sociable element. In the early days of online meetings, training events and so on, a producer might have stayed entirely in the background, dealing quietly with technical issues and assisting participants to join and leave the session smoothly.

These days, a producer may be required to play a more 'upfront' role, sometimes leading parts of the sessions themselves, and at least contributing to the discussion at certain points. For this reason, a producer is sometimes now also referred to as host, moderator or assistant facilitator.

The relationship between the producer and the facilitator is a key aspect of the success (or not) of the virtual event, and this cannot be emphasised enough. They have to get on, of course, and understand how the other works, on top of being familiar with the content and structure of the session itself. It is noticeable in our experience that when a producer and facilitator 'duo' have worked together over a long period of time, the 'flow' of the session goes really well, with an implicit understanding of what is needed from each at any given moment. Such sessions are seamless and also generally the most useful and enjoyable for attendees.

More on this below, but for now, here is a list of tasks that might be expected of any producer supporting online training, coaching or meeting events on any scale.

What the facilitator can expect from the producer

We started this chapter with a (fictional) job advertisement for an online producer, and we will finish it by adding some details. Here are some of the key skills and abilities to look for when seeking out a producer to support you.

Technical knowledge

As we have seen, most of a producer's tasks and responsibilities relate to the technicalities of running a virtual meeting, session or event. However, while it can be useful indeed to have the company's technical 'whizz-kid' as the producer, anyone who is usually not afraid of learning something new and understands the basics of working online can actually learn to fulfil this much-needed and back-up role. Most platforms that are built for online meetings and trainings are designed to be user-friendly and thus (in theory at least) easy to learn.

Solution-focused and practical

The producer will need to explore and learn all the 'ins' and 'outs' of the platform that you're using. S/he will need to know under which menu you can find certain features or settings. There may be little time during sessions when problems or questions arise to do this, so agility and speed in finding solutions is important. Furthermore, questions that the participants ask about the platform, and its tools, may also need to be answered by the producer, unless the facilitator has the knowledge to cover this.

Calm and relaxed under pressure

With a group of new users that are inexperienced working online, or with unexpected disconnections and people needing help, it can get rather hectic at times in the producer's corner! S/he will therefore need to stay calm under pressure and keep focus on steadily helping everyone to reconnect, whilst being able to answer any technical questions. This is no easy task, and requires focus and good skills in managing pressure. A producer who can remain confident and composed at all times makes a huge positive difference to participants' confidence, and the facilitator's delivery.

All that said, it's important to recognise that even the most gifted producer cannot work magic. Any producer has their limits when it comes to solving problems. There is only so much a producer can do at times when a number of major challenges arise at the same time, which is why it is often helpful for the facilitator also to have a certain level of technical knowledge as back-up.

A comforting and reassuring presence

 Much of what a producer does in any session is talk through specific challenges with participants, sometimes 'live' in the session itself, but also via email or phone behind the scenes. This not only requires the producer to be knowledgeable and reassuring in order to stop participants from getting anxious when things go wrong, it also requires superior communication skills, both verbal and in writing.

Content knowledge and ability to improvise

Of course it is very important that the producer should know the 'content' of the session and have had a chance to rehearse it with the facilitator beforehand. It is just as important for the producer to be able to improvise, or 'wing it', when there are unexpected interruptions and diversions from the agenda or training plan. We have known producers step in and take over an activity when the facilitator was experiencing ongoing audio problems, or lost their Internet connection for some minutes.

Awareness and familiarity with the facilitator's 'approach'

Throughout this book, we refer to the kinds of communication principles and practical 'ground rules' that an online facilitator may introduce to make the session successful, and to give it his or her own unique flavour. This is an important aspect of the facilitator's approach, and a producer needs to be familiar with, and adjust to these, in order to make the session flow well.

For example, the degree of control a facilitator wishes to take in her session. A facilitator who is willing to 'go with the flow' and keep the agenda flexible is likely to create a very different kind of mood or atmosphere in session than one with a tightly-planned agenda and little room for spontaneity. The producer should know what to expect in order to support the facilitator in using their strengths and skills most productively.

Versatility and willingness to practise

In online production, as in many things, experience is key – a fledgling producer needs to practice to become proficient. And alongside experience, comes versatility. Every producer should try out a different role from time to time – whether participating in, or presenting, the occasional session – in order to experience the possibilities as well as the limitations of the online platform from another viewpoint.

Be proactive in professional development

Finally, the willingness to constantly learn and develop as a producer, at any level of experience, is crucial. Technology is changing all the time, and so are the nature and possibilities offered by virtual sessions. Any producer who simply wants to stick to what s/he knows, and not move with the times, will find themselves behind the times very quickly and in danger of becoming out of touch.

Production Tasks – Before the Session

Scheduling the sessions

A session needs to be scheduled, whichever technology platform you are using. The producer will need to schedule it precisely, taking into account any time-zone differences for attendees (and also, as our anecdote at the start of this chapter illustrates, what is humanly possible for the tired facilitator!)

When scheduling the session, the producer can opt to select certain settings, for example whether or not the use of a webcam will be available during the session, or whether participants will be allowed to 'annotate' (write notes or even drawings on the slides or whiteboards shown) during the session. These are points to be decided at design stage, of course, before scheduling takes place.

Conducting technical checks

We strongly advise that a technical check should be conducted with all your participants before the first session, to sort out any potential connection and audio problems in advance, for example, so that the session itself is not disrupted for the whole group.

We arrange a quick 'technical check' with each individual participant via our producer/s at least a week in advance of the session itself, by arranging to 'connect' on the relevant platform in order to 'troubleshoot' any problems that occur at that point. This kind of check might only take a few minutes and of course can easily be done by the producer. Apart from minimising disruption, it helps attendees who are new to virtual sessions to feel comfortable and relaxed in the knowledge that they can make a smooth connection for the session itself.

Sending technical information and producer's contact details

It's a great idea to make sure your participants come prepared to your virtual sessions. What this means is avoiding spending too much time on 'getting to know the platform' instead of getting your training started.

While we always plan some time for familiarisation with the platform in our opening or 'Kick Off' session, if it's a programme rather than a stand-alone event, it is important to cover the basics in advance. To do this, we send our participants a short guidebook or instruction video (see **Resources** section, 2.2) to get familiar with the platform a few weeks in advance, so that they have the chance to prepare for the live session in their own time and be ready to interact and get involved.

At some point in the past, even the most experienced facilitator was a complete beginner and it helps to remember how daunting it can be the very first time you join a live session. No wonder many new attendees revert almost automatically to 'sitting on mute' if they feel less than confident with the technology. We also let the participants have the producer's contact details in advance of the session, so they can get in touch with any questions they may have.

Sending joining information for each session
The producer will send out the link participants need to log in to the session, with clear instructions and with his or her contact details. This allows people to get in touch quickly and easily if they are not able to login to the meeting platform.

Of course, it's important to remember that participants' experience with the technology can vary enormously. Some will be experienced users and will easily connect, while others may be completely new to the experience of 'meeting' via an online platform and will therefore need a guiding hand in finding the right buttons, telephone numbers or headset plug-in points. Any challenges such as these can be swiftly ironed out by a competent and calm producer to help the facilitator.

Preparing content/activities
Before a session starts, a producer can be very helpful to facilitators in assisting with the preparation of presentations, polls, quizzes and evaluations. At the start of a session, he or she can upload the proper documents, prepare all online content and URLs and have it to hand during the session. This of course saves a considerable amount of time and prevents awkward delays in the session later.

For this purpose we recommend that you work with a 'script' where all information for both the facilitator and the producer is stored – you can find more information on script formats below. The script is a technical guide to the session, including content/key topics, how these will be delivered, and who by, as well as the pre-work required by producer and facilitator. It gives timings and the order of activities in the session, but it most certainly should not be a word-for-word document from which the facilitator reads. We give more information on script formats below and there is a sample under *'Resources'* 3.1.

Production Tasks – During the Session

Managing the start of the session

As you might imagine, the producer is usually very active at the start of each session getting everyone 'in' on time. S/he will keep a sharp eye on the status of the attendees that are coming in, and on the chat box, his or her email Inbox and also have a telephone to hand. The beginning of a session is often very 'full on' for a producer, who may be (often at the same time) chatting to people in chat-space who seem to be having trouble with their audio, or re-sending links to those who are late joining, sometimes even emailing or calling them if they have not joined after several minutes.

A producer can quickly resend session log-in details if required, as s/he will have all participants' contact details at hand. While the facilitator can welcome those that have already logged in, the producer can quietly do their supporting job in the background, hardly noticed by the group.

Helping people feel instantly 'at home' in the session

In comparison to entering a live training venue, entering the virtual training or meeting 'room' can be a bit awkward, especially for the first time. There is no coffee machine or comfortable chairs, where participants can informally chat with their fellow attendees, getting acquainted or catching up socially.

Participants joining a virtual session, especially for the first time, can sometimes therefore feel uncomfortable. What to do – speak or not speak? Introduce yourself or not? Go on mute, or contribute to the conversation? To avoid this kind of uneasy beginning, the facilitator or the producer can actively welcome people in a friendly and chatty way, and promote what we call a 'virtual coffee corner' atmosphere to start up the informal interaction between attendees.

We do this in different ways, sometimes via an introductory slide which sets the mood of the meeting – it often actually shows coffee cups or a cafe space somewhere in the world, or something else which suggests a relaxed, chatty atmosphere. Usually the facilitator and/or producer are themselves chatting to various people as they join, and we prefer this to any kind of formal introduction and specifically ask people to stay audible/unmuted, unless there is considerable disruptive background noise.

It helps to remember that this kind of relaxed, friendly and informal atmosphere is very helpful in enabling people to build relationships swiftly, so that they can communicate with each other and learn in interactive enjoyment rather than nervous silence.

Helping late attendees to join and fit in smoothly

Once the facilitator has started the session, it can be quite disruptive if people log in late. The producer can do a lot to minimise this disruption by contacting any latecomers via the chat-box and bringing them up to speed on the content covered so far, or helping them with login issues.

Helping people get to know the virtual meeting space

Once people have joined successfully, they are likely to need some further support discovering and getting to know the platform's features, and managing any technical mishaps that may arise, if they are a group of people that have never used any kind of online platform before. This is often the case, whether or not they have received the technical information/manual sent in advance of the session, helpful though that is.

The producer can help people with any such difficulties using the 'chat' function privately with the relevant person, without other participants being interrupted. This might mean helping them find the right buttons to click, work the sliders to adjust their audio levels, or find the right phone number to dial, and so on.

Managing and supporting guest speakers and others

Sometimes a specific topic is addressed for which an expert is invited to act as a guest speaker. He or she may or may not be experienced with a virtual platform and may need extra help logging in and using the features. A producer can help out, while the lead facilitator continues with the session. As with all participants, it is advised for guest speakers to do a 'tech check' and prepare for using the online platform well in advance of the actual session.

Keeping people busy when something goes wrong

Even with the best will in the world, and plenty of preparation, technical matters can and do take up time. We're used to this in the face to face classroom – the slow upload of PowerPoint slides, say, or the laptop or projector that doesn't want to work. We're used to it, and we often forgive it because we have other things to look at and do when we are sitting together with others.

In virtual space, that is sometimes not the case. If you are asking people to keep their attention fixed on their computer screen, you can hardly be surprised when they become bored or irritated if the screen goes blank, leaving them with little else to do other than to drum their fingers, check their emails, or – at worst – wonder why they joined the session in the first place.

Here, again, a producer is an invaluable source of support. In many facilitator-producer pairings, it is agreed that when an issue arises that affects most of the people in the group, the producer may step in to sort it out while the other finds an appropriate 'filler' activity to keep people engaged and motivated. That filler activity may range from exercises such as brainstorming ideas on a whiteboard, through to organising an online sing-along (yes, it's been known!). It's much easier, of course, to anticipate and prevent people being disengaged than it is to 'win back' their attention, once lost. A sample 'filler' activity is provided in the resources section.

MANAGING TECHNICAL ASPECTS OF IN-SESSION ACTIVITIES

There are numerous ways in which a producer can help the facilitator with specific activities before and during the session. These include:

- Setting up and launching breakout rooms

- Creating and launching polls

- Sharing web content, quizzes, videos, survey results, and so forth.

- Saving notes and annotations. In an interactive session where attendees are asked to annotate or create documents – for example, whiteboard annotations in breakout groups – the producer can make sure all the information is stored for use as required both during, or after, the session.

- Recording the sessions or meetings. Online sessions can be recorded, allowing people to look back at the session that they took part in, or to watch/listen to it in their own time when they have missed the live session. The producer can start and end the recording, and is also able to make a rough edit of it and supply a link to the online recording which can be distributed after the session to all participants.

Managing time

During longer sessions of 90 minutes or more, where there is a break halfway and people are advised to move away from their computer for a few minutes, the producer can pull up a countdown clock or timer, so everyone can see at a glance when they need to be back at their screen. Producers can also assist a facilitator to keep track of time during specific exercises, such as breakouts, or during the main session itself.

Keeping time in short, focused virtual sessions and meetings can often be tough and the producer is a particularly useful resource here.

Feeding questions to the facilitator

The Q&A feature is especially useful in virtual sessions for bigger groups, where the number of attendees is too large for spontaneous interaction. Here you can use the Q&A function to answer questions, and have the producer give the answers directly via the Q&A window. The producer may also function as a 'filter' to pick out certain relevant questions that are then forwarded to the facilitator to discuss aloud.

Communicating with the facilitator

We put this last but it is most certainly not at all 'least', in terms of a producer's priorities. Whilst doing everything outlined above, s/he needs to keep the facilitator informed throughout the session on the status of all attendees, notifying him or her if anyone has suddenly lost their connection, or cannot respond to questions because their audio is failing, and so on.

This means that the facilitator also keeps an eye on the chat-box, so that there are no awkward silences when (for example) a participant who has been experiencing audio problems for 5 minutes is invited to speak – and the rest is silence. If the facilitator is kept up-to-date by the producer, this can be managed smoothly and calmly until the person is back in session with audio working fully.

Production Tasks – After the Session

Point of contact for asynchronous ('out of session') activities

If you are delivering an ongoing training programme, say, or series of learning events or meetings, it is often helpful, if not essential, to incorporate some activities that are done in participants' own time – asynchronously – rather than take up time with them in live sessions, which should be more focused on group activities and discussions.

Examples of asynchronous activities include background reading on relevant topics, completing questionnaires, tests, quizzes and surveys, preparing slides or other documents to share in the session – and so on. The producer may be the first point of contact for participants with any questions between sessions, and also the person who communicates individual asynchronous activities and homework to all participants.

Having one point of contact keeps things simple for participants. In many cases, our producers also set up and maintain the group's own site in the e-learning environment where a record of sessions, recordings, minutes or notes of meetings, a summary of homework/action points and any other related activities is available to the group's eyes only. Here participants can access the session itself via the **relevant** link – a simple and quicker process than checking through inboxes to find the email invitation.

Managing the close of a learning programme

There are usually various tasks to fulfil at the completion of a series of virtual meetings or events. After a training programme is over, there may be certification documents and evaluation forms to distribute, for example, and/or marketing literature to keep attendees engaged with your topic.

When you do NOT need a producer

Of course, that is not to say that you, as a facilitator, will always need a producer's help and support. There are likely to be numerous occasions when you don't

- When you are working one to one, in individual coaching
- When you are working with a very small group (say, 3 or 4 people) who are experienced with online meetings and know how to get beyond technical 'glitches' without assistance

- When the technology used is so straightforward and understood by all that there is no need for any technical or administrative back-up

- In a highly informal, 'one off' meeting between colleagues where there is little pressure of time and the intention is mainly sociable rather than structured towards achieving certain goals.

Working together as a team

The facilitator/producer teams we work with have very often never met face to face – not only because they may live and work whole continents apart, but also because in our experience it is completely possible to work as a tight team with a producer you have never physically met It really is not necessary to be in the same building, although of course some teams are.

Here are some important considerations in working effectively with a producer.

Invest time in the collaborative relationship
Firstly, while each partnership is unique, each becomes effective only after some solid practice together, and discussion of needs and expectations in order to establish trust. While it is entirely possible to work with a new producer for the first time and still manage the session together perfectly well – the best results usually come from a longer-standing collaborative relationship.

Expect, and plan for, some 'overlap' of responsibilities
The producer and facilitator roles need to be distinct, and responsibilities clear. However, there is almost always going to be a certain area of overlap, especially in highly interactive sessions where there is a lot of free-flowing dialogue and a degree of spontaneity within the structure.

This means that although any good producer should back up the facilitator technically as much as possible, it will always be important for the facilitator to have a basic comprehension of the technology. Conversely, the producer may need to step in on various occasions and lead the facilitation when the facilitator is unable to, and to add variety. There may also be a role for the producer to liven up the session if engagement from participants is low. For instance, answering a question from the facilitator when there is no response from the group. These are items to discuss and clarify before working together.

Work out your preparation 'timeline' together

It helps to establish a 'standard approach' to preparation and delivery, with clear roles and responsibilities. That way, no preparation elements for the sessions will be overlooked.

Use a (shared) script and checklist 'templates'

Streamline the process further by using checklists for all preparation steps and the required actions and tasks for the start-up of the session itself. As already stated, the script is not a 'word for word' presentation but should give details of preparation/ production 'pre-work' for each session, and a list of activities, timings and roles/ responsibilities during the session

The trainer or facilitator prepares the script according to the programme's design and specified objectives, and the producer can add URL links or any other information s/ he needs to have at hand during the session. A sample script is included within the **Resource list** at the back of this book.

The way you lay out the script will depend on the kind of session you are running.

A meeting will require less structure than a training event, so that a loose note of agenda items, timings, and who is speaking to each item, could well be adequate – nothing fancy required. But if you are running an activity-packed training or team coaching session to a tight timeline, you will need to have a more structured and detailed script handy.

Rehearse together...

In preparation for any newly designed session with a producer it makes sense to do a run-through or 'rehearsal' first. This is a great way to find out any logistical or technical obstacles, and unforeseen problems. There may also be a guest speaker or co-trainer who needs time to get used to the online platform at a relaxed pace and with no audience present.

Even with a rehearsal, we recommend planning for each facilitator/producer pair to 'meet' online at least 40 minutes before the start of the session, to go through the script and ensure all relevant slides and other files and activities are uploaded, and ready to go.

... But do not over-prepare

What does over-preparation look like? It means – for example – preparing so many notes on what you will say and what should happen that, when looking at your notes during the session, you cannot see the main points or the flow of the session in a sea of text. Over preparation is trying to 'learn the script by heart', like a role in a play.

If you do, you will not only sound mechanical and unrelaxed – people can always tell, even without webcam, when you are reading from a script – but you will also find it difficult to cope when interruptions occur. No trainer worth their fee would ever 'script read' in a face to face session, so avoid it in online delivery too.

By now, you will have some clarity about the technological and human support that the producer can provide. In the next chapter, we start looking at the sessions themselves – their content and the best design options in different contexts and for varying client needs.

LEARNING THEORY AND DESIGN OF VIRTUAL EVENTS

4

by Mara Garofalo and Fredrik Fogelberg

The difference between 'webinars' and 'web-based learning'

Have you ever attended a webinar or an online event? Have you ever felt bored and that you were wasting your time? After all, you could have just read about what was being discussed or presented in a book.

When asking people 'what is an online meeting?', the response that you may often get is that it's a webinar. However, webinars are only one way to share knowledge and information on key topics. Real virtual collaboration (or facilitation) is about learning together in a collaborative way.

Nowadays, technology provides the possibility to collaborate through web platforms such as Adobe Connect, GoToMeeting, Lync, WebEx and others. The big difference between webinars and web-based learning is interactivity, and in this chapter we will describe current adult learning theories, and how they highlight the connections between interaction or participation and effective learning through web-based synchronous meetings.

The virtual classroom has certain specific elements that need to be taken into account and respected, in order to use them effectively so as to engage participants through constant and meaningful interaction.

Virtual 'live' learning: the theories behind the practice

So, let's look at some of the theories behind the practice of live synchronous learning sessions. Current theories of adult learning emphasise the importance of building on the learner's experience, to develop 'meaningful' knowledge, through interaction with other learners (Wicks, 2009).

It's clear how learning in a synchronous virtual classroom is not so different from that idea. The process of learning 'virtually' involves similar kinds of activities as those used in face-to-face learning, except that – and this is really important in the design of virtual sessions and programmes – participants' attention span is very much shorter in virtual space. This fact obviously has consequences for the learning process, and thus for the design of virtual events.

In his review of adult learning theories, Huang (2002) explained that 'constructivist' theories deriving from the earlier work of Dewey and Piaget, state that learners 'construct' and test new knowledge based on their own prior experience. Following this idea, 'knowledge' is therefore connected in learners' minds with their own experience in order to explore and make sense of it, and also then often focused on solving real life problems. From this perspective we can see the emerging value of 'experiential learning' – linking ideas with experience, and putting them to work in daily life.

Vygotsky (1978, cited in Huang 2002) stresses the importance of the 'social context' in learning, the interaction and growing relationships between learners and the instructor, or facilitator. In this theory, as with experiential learning, the learning process is based upon exploration of individual learners' needs and goals, and is facilitated by the instructor through activities and constant interaction. This sounds, and is, very different from any notion of a 'one way, monologue-style' delivery, bringing to mind a classroom teacher telling students key points to note down.

According to Malcolm Knowles (1984), who coined the term "andragogy" as "the art and science of helping adults learn", the adult learner appreciates being autonomous in choosing what to learn and how to do it, developing self-directedness and building on her own experiences. In addition, the adult will learn because of internal factors motivating him or her and the need for practical application to solve problems or gaps. In Knowles' view, adults are very much hands-on in their learning processes.

Brookfield identified two elements of adult learning that help participants to interact in synchronous learning: experiential learning (based on adults' experiences) – as discussed briefly above – and dialogic methods of instruction, (based on circular communication). Such methods may have a profound effect, according to some commentators. 'Transformative Learning Theory', represented by Mezirow (1990 cited in Murugiah 2005) states that learning encourages us to change old thinking through critical reflection and debate .

From these key themes in adult learning, we can easily see that the adult educator needs to ensure that the conditions for supporting effective learning and creating motivation are established from the outset. For the virtual facilitator what this means practically is setting a cooperative climate where the learner's needs and interests will be taken into account.

The Virtual Classroom: an interactive space for co-creation

The guidelines that emerge from these learning theories provide an excellent basis to help you design virtual training and coaching sessions and events for live, synchronous delivery. After all, virtual facilitation is about designing a structured environment conducive to learning and not – as we have pointed out already – about technology.

Of course technology is a tool, and a highly valuable tool, to maximise learning, but it is a means to an end, and so learning all about the technology is not (usually) the end in itself. Designing a course for virtual synchronous delivery requires a number of skills beyond technological proficiency, and these are, as you might expect, also already required in face-to-face course design.

The difference is that working in virtual space, we need to develop additional skills relating to group dynamics and distance learning as well as of course getting to grips with the main characteristics of the technology provided in the platform used.

Characteristics of the virtual classroom environment

The most important difference between conventional training and the virtual classroom is that you generally do not see your audience! As a facilitator, you hear, and listen to all the cues, silence included. When you cannot see participants, it is imperative to make them individually "visible". You need to ensure that every participant is heard, that they take their space and position themselves in the group.

A powerful and simple way to do this is through the 'Check in' process, an introductory activity where each participant in the session is given the opportunity to express their feelings, state of mind, and expectations about the session which is about to start. Typically, it is just like a "tour de table", one participant starting the round and passing the turn on to another participant of his choice until everyone has spoken. It is easy to notice the change in atmosphere during the check in process, with participants showing more comfort with the group, more openness in their contributions and an increased level of trust.

To see or not to see?

Opinions differ on the value of using webcams during virtual training. Though it might be worthwhile to make use of real time video because it can help in creating more closeness in the group, continuous use of webcams easily becomes distracting and therefore counter-productive. Webcams can be used during check in, or during specific exercises, but 'overuse' often creates difficulties due to quality of the image, unwanted fidgeting and delay between voice and visual (Hofmann, 2010).

People tend to resist the idea that trust can be built in a virtual environment – that is, without actually physically meeting one another. Research (Caulat, 2006) has contradicted this, and so has my own experience as a practitioner. Comments from participants in our courses reflect the idea that people working together do not necessarily need to build a face-to-face relationship to build trust. See the text box for an example.

BUILDING TRUST AND COLLABORATION REMOTELY IN A VIRTUAL TEAM

As a virtual facilitator, I was collaborating actively with a virtual team. I only knew one person prior to starting the adventure! The other three members, producers and coordinator, where located in another country, and we used email and Dropbox to exchange documents and comments, telephone and Skype to discuss things over, SMS and IMs to deliver urgent messages and requests, and Webex to share and modify presentations and scripts collaboratively. Each of our team meetings and bilateral meetings started with an update on our lives and things we were busy doing.

Continued...

Continued from overpage

We joked, challenged each other and shared personal facts and stories. And we did not physically meet until after having worked together for three full years!

The work was always done and we totally relied on one another for the delivery. No hesitation. We really trusted each other and the trust was built virtually, through addressing common objectives and allowing ourselves to speak up and present our views even if different from the others'. Building trust virtually may take some time, because participants in a learning cohort need to get acquainted with one another and move from being there at the same time, to doing collaboratively.

Synchronous or asynchronous?

The classroom as we know it is no longer. The Virtual classroom is a technological assembly of people located remotely from each other, with a variety of learning styles and interests. However, they all have one thing in common: they are busy and do not want to waste their time.

In order for synchronous learning to be effective and meaningful it has to be necessary. What I mean by that is that if what you are going to teach your audience can be done asynchronously, it should not be included in the virtual synchronous session, but presented as pre-work or as an assignment. When sitting in front of a computer with headphones on, listening to long lectures from the facilitator, people simply get utterly bored – and they will use their time in their 'known' effective way, looking at their emails for example. And then, as a facilitator, you have lost them.

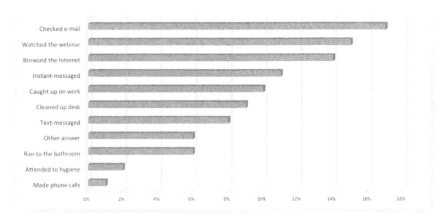

Engaging your participants

How to ensure that you engage attendees? Keep them busy! Include activities in your design that call for their participation, that tickle their curiosity and are meaningful in relation to their background, interests, learning needs and practical applications.

When we train and facilitate face-to-face, we alternate between input from the facilitator and individual or group activities. In the virtual classroom you need to do the same, only at a different pace. The facilitator's input should be limited in length; we suggest chunks of maximum 5 minutes each. Remember what we said earlier: what can be delivered asynchronously should not be delivered synchronously.

Building on the adult learning theories we described earlier in this chapter, adults attending virtual courses very often expect to learn something that is meaningful and directly useful and applicable. They benefit most from courses designed as highly interactive and adapted to their needs and interests.

What this suggests is that virtual courses should be designed around the content one wants to deliver, but also that space should be allocated for participants to drive the session in the direction that most suits them, within the boundaries of the subject. This is what we call finding the balance between order and (relatively speaking, at least) chaos!

In other words, if we want to facilitate self-directed learning that is meaningful and relevant to participants, we as facilitators need to be ready to follow the lead of learners – both in adapting to their pace, and in exploring topics to a depth that is suitable for them.

In the next section below we explore the design process, as shown here in two key phases:

- Discovery phase
  - Data gathering
  - Presenting results & recommendations
- Design phase

The next two phases are the delivery and evaluation phases. Delivery is the focus of **Chapter Five** which offers practical tips, tools and ideas to create a powerful, effective presence when working virtually.

Virtual Design Process: the Discovery Phase

Data gathering

Let's use an example. Your client, internal or external, requests you to design and deliver a training module on leading effective on-line meetings. At first, as in any Training Needs Assessment, you will need to explore the explicit learning need as defined by the client. This means gathering data from a variety of sources, both on the learning need and the context in which it arises – in other words, what background factors within the client organisation/s are creating this need

Here are some of the people you are likely to approach for more information:

- The person who has contacted you (the 'client') – by interview

- Representatives from the target audience (participants), by interview or survey. Interviews can be done either individually or in a group

- Key stakeholders in the organisation, such as senior managers, senior employees with extensive experience, new employees, critical thinkers (who may object to the idea of this training), internal or external customers, union or worker's council representatives.

The more variety of perspective, the more likely the training will be to address not just the explicit needs but also the 'implicit' ones of various stakeholder groups, with a considerable positive effect on the impact the training can then deliver.

Presenting results and recommendations to the client

Results of the 'discovery', or research, phase of the design are presented back to the client, with recommendations for next steps. One of the possible recommendations is always to not proceed with the training or a different type of intervention from what the client has asked for. In particular situations, such as when the 'implicit' need is different from the explicit one, training may not be called for.

To take an obvious example, if the organisation does not have a web meeting platform in place that is easily accessible to employees, a training programme in web meetings may not be the best solution at the time. This may sound obvious, but in reality the timing of development interventions is often ill-chosen or other factors in the organisation are not in place.

SAMPLE INTERVIEW QUESTIONS FOR DISCOVERY PHASE

Exploring the rationale for training

- Why do you need this training?
- Why is it needed now?
- What problem/s will this intervention address?
- What change do you expect to see happening after this intervention?
- What might happen if this training did not take place?
- Where is the 'pain' that needs to be resolved?

Exploring the organisational need/s behind the training request

- How is this training connected to the strategy of the organisation?
- What other ways are there to reach the desired impact?
- What obstacles are there to its success?

Sponsorship and backing from stakeholders

- Who has asked for this training?
- Who might be against it?
- How committed is senior management to this training programme and how can we involve them to show their commitment?

Exploring what makes the target group 'tick'

- What is the motivation of the target audience?
- What is their level of knowledge/ expertise in the area of this topic?
- How familiar are they with the learning technology?

- How much time is there for this programme to be delivered, and will participants be willing to take that time away from their work?
- What type of training has not worked here in the past? What irritates people?
- What type of training has worked well here in the past? What makes people happy?

Applying the learning in practice after the programme

- What else needs to happen to strengthen the impact of the training?
- What would help them to benefit most from this programme?
- How can their managers help to support implementation for the learnings?
- What support or tools need to be in place for the learners to implement their new learnings?
- How will the new behaviours be rewarded?
- How will the impact of this intervention be measured?

Practical concerns

- What technology is in place for this type of training?
- Do all learners know how to use it?
- Where can they get support with the technology?
- What is the budget for the training?

Virtual Design Process: the Design Phase

Once you have reached agreement with your client about objectives, the target audience, the timing, budget, technology, embedding it in the organisation, involvement of relevant managers and devised an evaluation process – it is time to start the 'real' design work!

During the discovery phase (as you will have noticed), there is considerable overlap with what we might consider a classic, face to face training process. In the design phase however, the difference between design for face to face sessions and virtual ones are considerably bigger.

The virtual classroom is a place for co-creating learning, and each participant will take from it a learning experience and insights that can be useful, meaningful and entirely applicable to his or her specific needs. And that is the beauty of it. If designed to address the needs of the participants, and not the facilitator's need to take control, virtual learning becomes a very powerful tool indeed.

Start with the objectives and define session content accordingly

The overall objective will dictate the choice of content for each session. However, be aware that the amount of content in a virtual session is, at most, about 50% of what you can teach in a face to face session. Virtual sessions are an excellent environment for interactive and experiential learning, very much in line with adult learning theories discussed earlier. Working synchronously with others in virtual space is, however, far less suited for 'lecture'-style learning.

The overall objective will dictate the choice of content for each session. In our example, the objective might be 'participants will be able to chair teleconferences in an effective and engaging manner'. Based on this, we might create four virtual sessions of two hours each, with the following content:

Session 1
Kick off
Virtual etiquette
*Platform:
WebEx*

Session 2
Choosing your
technology
*Platform:
WebEx*

Session 3
Virtual Meeting
techniques
*Platform:
Phone conference*

Session 4
Engagement
and trust
*Platform:
Lync*

- Live Virtual Training sessions
- Individual assignments *(asynchronous)*

Furthermore, time is always limited in virtual sessions. It is important not to 'overpromise' to your client about the amount of cognitive content you can deliver in the virtual classroom. Knowledge, information or 'content' is best taught asynchronously, for instance in an e-learning environment, and this is where reading, writing, and memorising information fits in well. Examples of asynchronous learning technologies include reading e-documents, downloading a video tutorial in your own time, playing back the recording of a live session that's already taken place – and there are numerous others. The point is, it's in your own time and you can 'take in' the information at a pace that suits you.

Overall, the synchronous session is about facilitating learning for participants through discussion, interaction and sharing ideas 'in the moment'.

'Hands-on' design

Now it's time to fill individual sessions with content and activities. For this, we have created a set of 'Ten Commandments' for designing virtual events.

THE TEN COMMANDMENTS FOR VIRTUAL SYNCHRONOUS DESIGN

1. Work from the strengths of virtual communication, not its shortcomings

2. Interactivity, interactivity

3. Use features to engage participants

4. Address the social aspect

5. Provide structure and clarity

6. Apply a virtual etiquette

7. Keep it short and use energy breaks

8. Use virtual 'breakout' rooms

9. Use images over words

10. Give opportunities to practise

Let's review each of these 'Ten Commandments' in detail:

The first commandment: work from the strengths of virtual communication, not its shortcomings. Design from the perspective that virtual facilitation is a powerful tool with its own great advantages, and not the second best choice.

The second commandment: Interactivity, interactivity

The 3 most important design elements are interactivity, interactivity and interactivity. Remember that people learn by doing; the facilitator's input should be brief and focused and (inter)activity should be provided frequently.

The 'rule of thumb' we follow is that after every 3 to 5 minutes of input, an exercise should be included in the design. It could be a discussion on the topic at hand, using the whiteboard; or a game; a small group 'debate'; a poll or any other activity you might find useful to engage participants. The sky is (almost) the limit! Indeed, we would argue that there are even more possibilities for interactivity than in a classic classroom.

So designing for interaction in a nutshell means asking yourself the following questions:

- What features of the platform have you not used yet?

- How can you as facilitator complement and support participants' learning in a creative and (at times) spontaneous way?

- How can you best invite your audience to think through the ideas that are shared, and then translate them into practical actions?

The third commandment: Use features for engaging participants

Make use of the tools and features provided by the platform. Most of the well-known platforms offer at least the following features:

- Whiteboards

- File sharing

- Annotation tools (drawing, writing, pointing)

- Emoticons

- Chat box

- Video

- Sharing websites

- Polls

- Question & Answer tool.

These features can and should be included in the design as an encouragement to participation, and, depending on the type of group, can be surprisingly effective in engaging the 'less verbal' participants. This is an instance where the virtual classroom often outperforms the traditional face to face environment – the plethora of tools and features available, used well, are a powerful and exciting combination to engage participants' curiosity and encourage a mood of playful experimentation. And if children learn through play and experimentation, why not adults also?

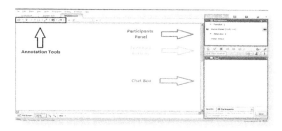

Screenshot of a WebEx participant screen showing annotation tools, participant panel, feedback buttons and chat box.

The fourth commandment: Address the social aspect

For a group of people – especially if they are strangers to each other – to learn collaboratively, we need to build trust and create closeness first. By making participants feel comfortable with one another we ensure they will participate more fully and be engaged. This, in turn, leads to a more powerful and valuable learning experience.

Sample activities:

Check in: the main purpose of this activity is to allow each participant to be aware of their own presence and that of others in the meeting or training session. This technique is rooted in the principle of foreground and background from Gestalt Psychology (Perls, 1973). A question is proposed and each participant is requested to answer briefly, and in turn – giving him/her the opportunity to be heard early on in the session. As stated earlier, the Check In is a great opportunity for people to talk about what is in the foreground for them and to be included in the virtual group. It is this kind of personal information that creates understanding, comfort and trust.

Check in

What's in the foreground – physical, mental, emotional

And I pass on to ....

Check out: A process at the end of a synchronous session where the facilitator asks each participant to briefly share how she has experienced the meeting and (for example) any particular ideas or activities that have been useful or thought-provoking. Again, this is not a long speech, but an attempt to give closure to the time spent together, and to provide a space for each individual to share impressions and say goodbye.

Icebreakers encouraging a degree of personal disclosure and helping re-energise the group. A sample ice-breaker is described in the text box.

LITTLE KNOWN FACTS: AN ICEBREAKER TO BUILD 'VIRTUAL CLOSENESS'

The activity is simple and fun, allowing participants to share a fact about themselves that other participants would not normally know. It does not have to be too personal, but it is often something original or humorous. The participants send it to the producer who lists the little known facts on a slide. Next the participants guess which fact is about which participant.

The fifth commandment: Provide structure and clarity

First structure, then play. Setting clear boundaries (time given to an activity, the task to be carried out and the role each person will play within it) provides a healthy group dynamic which helps to accomplish the task. A clear objective, structure and ground rules are essential for creating an effective learning environment.

In our live sessions, we will always outline the objectives and an agenda for the session. Within this, we will also make clear where there is space for flexibility, and also help participants understand how we would like them to communicate and participate in the activities that are outlined. This is helpful both because, if they know what's expected of them, participants are generally better placed to work with the facilitator and keep to time – and because knowing what you are going to be doing is even more reassuring in virtual space than it is in the face to face classroom. Feeling clueless about the agenda of course has the opposite effect.

Type of activities:

- Objective for the session
- Agenda for the sessions
- Review of previous learning.

The sixth commandment: Apply a virtual etiquette

We have already made some comments about the importance and impact of providing the 'groundrules' or 'virtual etiquette' within your session. Here are some examples to consider from some of the live sessions we have run.

Virtual Meeting Etiquette

Getting ready.....

1. Each team member joins from her/his own work space – no subgroups
2. Join the meeting from a quiet place
3. USB headset gives best audio quality
4. Cable is more stable than WiFi
5. Put a sign on your door that you are attending a virtual meeting/training

PLEASE
DO NOT
DISTURB

The seventh commandment: Keep it short and use energy breaks

Sessions should be kept relatively short and focused. Remember, people tend to choose virtual courses because of the flexibility they offer and the possibility of following them from almost anywhere in the world – without leaving your armchair! In general, we prefer to have sessions of two hours, three hours if absolutely essential.

Whatever the duration of the session, it is essential to add short breaks whenever sessions are longer than 90 minutes. Otherwise, attention and concentration become more difficult. Participants will be encouraged to get up and move away from their computers during these breaks and not stay at their screen to check emails or go on the web. It is astonishing to note just how much difference having a 5 minute break to refresh, have a drink, stretch and revive one's energy can make.

The eighth commandment: Use virtual breakout rooms

If a group has more than four or five participants, running a discussion in the plenary may not always offer everyone the opportunity for deeper reflection, especially (as often happens) the more extraverted personalities tend to dominate the conversations.

Which is why the 'breakout' room function available in many virtual platforms is an excellent way to support 'small group' activities where participants working in pairs or threes can have a more focused, in-depth discussion than 'at random' in a larger group.

Using the breakout groups function of your platform, the facilitator can assign questions to people to reflect on and discuss, saving their answers on a whiteboard, and returning to the plenary with the documents ready to share, just as you would in a face to face training session. In our experience, this adds tremendous value and is almost always appreciated by participants.

The breakout environment has the bonus of providing an intimate atmosphere and, as in most platforms it is not possible to record what is said there (as you might normally do in the main session). It offers a quiet, private space to share reflections and discuss topics in more depth. We prefer not to facilitate the breakout sessions, because it usually is not necessary, and standing back from doing so helps participants feel more engaged and in control of the discussion.

We are often surprised by how much more open and intimate the conversations in our virtual breakout spaces are! Participants may be ten time zones apart, but they experience a high degree of 'virtual closeness' when sitting together in an imaginary space, listening to each other's voices and working together on a joint task.

The ninth commandment: Use images over words

Think about the difference between using images and (written) words. While it will be important for the words you use – on slides, on whiteboards – to be clear , simple and easy to understand, you will be missing out on a very important resource if you do not include images in your presentational materials.

Why? If you provide text-heavy materials with too much written content, you'll hear silence – people reading, instead of listening and interacting. And the silence may be a bored silence, or a confused one – depending on whether your group are all equally able to speak the language you are using to deliver.

As much as possible, privilege the use of images over words. Limit the content to what is essential. Images are powerful conveyors of messages and trigger reflection, since they are often interpreted slightly different from learner to learner according to their own background and interests. Isn't there a popular saying: "an image is worth a thousand words"? In **Chapter Five** we talk more about the impact and imaginative possibilities of images in virtual space.

The tenth commandment: provide opportunities to practise

New knowledge needs to be meaningful and practical in order to be retained by the learner, and what makes it meaningful is being able to apply it. Make sure you create activities that are relevant to your participants' work, background, interests and that they allow for new concepts to be demonstrated and used. In some of our training programmes, we give each participant in turn the role of chairing the meeting, so they can practise on the spot what they have learnt.

In conclusion

This chapter has highlighted the vast possibilities of the virtual classroom and how to use them to create an interactive programme design. The smart virtual facilitator knows how to make the transition from the client's request to the virtual environment, using relevant features to offer maximum learning opportunities.

Well designed, an event in the virtual classroom can be even more effective than the same programme delivered in a classic classroom. Well-designed virtual events are engaging, energising, light-hearted and to the point; all at the same time.

And they make good use of participants' time and energy. Imagine the favour you are doing your group by saving them the time, money and effort they would have lost travelling to a common location. And, as we have seen, distance is no obstacle to group bonding: we have seen many groups where learners have become emotional during the last session when it was time to say goodbye.

The next chapter will discuss the facilitation process itself and how the facilitator can develop her of his unique style to make the most of these tools.

References

1) Murugiah, Santhiru S. (2005). Adult Learning Theories and their Application in Selecting the Functionality of Synchronous Learning Tools retrieved from http://eric.ed.gov/?id=ED492386

2) Corley, Mary Ann (2012). TEAL Center Fact Sheet No. 11: Adult Learning Theories, Adapted from the CALPRO Fact Sheet No. 5, Adult Learning Theories. https://teal.ed.gov/tealGuide/adultlearning

3) Hoffman, Jennifer (2010). Going Live in www.trainingmag.com. Nov-Dec 2010

4) Perls, Fritz (1973). The Gestalt approach

5) Knowles, Malcolm (1984). Andragogy in action: Applying modern principles of adult education. Jossey-Bass.

6) Caulat, Ghislaine (2006) Virtual Leadership. The Ashridge Journal

DEVELOPING YOUR OWN UNIQUE STYLE AND STRENGTHS AS A VIRTUAL FACILITATOR | 5

'Style is the perfection of a point of view'.
Richard Eberhart

Introduction: It's All About You (Baby)

So far in this book we have talked about what might be called the 'building blocks' or essentials of virtual facilitation that will help you to deliver a session or programme with flair and confidence. How to choose and master the technology that will support you best (without your stress level hitting the roof), how to work well with a producer, how to design training and sessions, or meetings, that will achieve the goals you and your client are focusing on – these are all important considerations before you get going as a virtual facilitator.

Now it's time to talk in more depth about what a facilitator actually does – the many tasks that arise before, during and after your session – as well as to explore with you the kinds of skills and qualities that enable successful facilitation. This chapter should provide you with plenty of information and practical tips about preparing and delivering enjoyable and successful virtual sessions on all kinds of topics.

This chapter covers a lot of ground, and so we've divided it into two broad sections. The first deals with the role and responsibilities, and the (seven) top skills and abilities that are generally required when you first start running sessions across distance. Practice and experience really does make perfect and after a number of sessions you will no longer need the sort of detailed checklists we offer here. It will all become natural, and instinctive.

This first half of the chapter is more useful reading if you are either a complete beginner, or with relatively limited experience, as a virtual facilitator. If you are more experienced, you may find it useful to skip this material, and turn to the second 'half' of this chapter, which is much more about you, and your intended impact in virtual space.

Here we introduce our 'VELVET' model for virtual facilitation, an acronym for six aspects of virtual facilitation you might consider in relation to yourself, and the way you like to work as a virtual facilitator.

While we know from our own experience that while there are very definitely certain **'rules', and principles** that will help to get you set up for success, we also know that there is no such thing as a single, universal approach to virtual communication. Just as in the face to face classroom, coaching session or meeting, each of us develops his or her own approach to virtual facilitation over time.

In this last section, we also suggest some **activities and further practical tips** that will help you develop your style and work on your challenges. Additional detail on these activities is included in the Resources section at the back of this book.

But let's begin with some basics: what the facilitator role involves, the key responsibilities you need to think about, and practical action points to help you on your way.

Role and responsibilities of a successful virtual facilitator

If you are in the position of recruiting a virtual facilitator for a live, online programme, you might find this list useful in setting out some key responsibilities, skills and qualities needed for the job.

Ensure the structure and delivery of the sessions meets the client's objectives. Of course this has to be at the top of the list, because if you don't achieve this, it doesn't matter how brilliantly energetic and engaging you are as a virtual facilitator, nor how interactive your delivery style, you will ultimately fail because your client will not be happy. In *Chapter Four* we talked about the discovery phase being that of 'scoping' out and researching client needs, and this goes without saying in virtual, just as in face to face facilitation.

One further point to add. At the time of writing, many business leaders required to receive training and/or coaching, work virtually more frequently than previously, yet are still unfamiliar with the multiple possibilities of virtual communication to achieve specific goals. Perhaps this is because their perspective has been influenced by having participated in too many 'one way' presentational webinars, or through sheer lack of familiarity with the technology.

Whatever the reason, you may need to take a little more time than usual to consider, and demonstrate, the different and innovative ways in which their needs can be met in a virtual session.

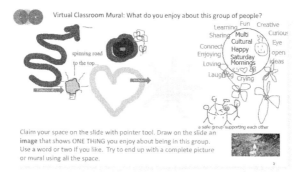

Interaction really is the name of the game.

Here we are, banging that drum again. But what does interaction actually look like in practice? There are many different ways of encouraging people to engage with each other and (ideally) to enjoy doing so. They include:

PRACTICAL TIPS

- Asking **questions and inviting** answers from everyone in the group

- Inviting people to **interrupt** freely, and to ask questions themselves when they wish

- Inviting people to **write responses to questions or comments on your slides or whiteboard** – what we call 'positive graffiti' (this really is something special to virtual facilitation – can you imagine writing on the facilitator's slide deck in the face to face training room? Or what might happen if scribbled on the slide screen at the front of the class?)

- Inviting people to **brainstorm ideas** via images or words on a whiteboard

- Organising **team games** where groups of participants work together to discuss and achieve specific aims

- Inviting people to use the **chat-space** freely throughout your session to engage with each other privately, and/or with the whole group as preferred

- Setting up **small group discussions** within the whole group, using breakout room technology for example

- Or split a group of ten or less into two and invite them to consider a case study and give their responses, one group talking while the other listens, then swopping around – this is called a 'virtual goldfish bowl'.

There's quite a list here, and many more things we could add. One or two of the techniques described here – the 'virtual goldfish bowl', for example – are described in more detail in *Resources* at the back of the book. And of course you will need to use any of these ideas from the perspective of what you need to achieve in the session, with purpose. Nothing you do as a virtual facilitator should be wasted – if participants get bored, you need to 'bring them back', but try to do so in a way that connects with the objectives of the session.

Communicate with the producer before, during and after the session.
We've covered the producer's role thoroughly in *Chapter Three*, and it will be no surprise to read here that the quality of the relationship with your technical back-up person, and your work to support it via constant communication at all times when working together is absolutely critical. Any facilitator working with a new producer for the first time would do well to make time to chat before the session – not only as a practical rehearsal for the session itself, but also to get to know him or her, and understand the way the producer likes to work .

Some producers like to stay muted and operate quietly behind the scenes, others prefer to be more actively involved and participate audibly in the session at specific moments. You need to know your producer's 'approach', and how to work well with her in the best interests of all participants. This is likely to include discussing how you communicate in the session – whether via chat space, aloud, via another platform like Skype, mobile phone when muted to participants – and so on.

Remember that much of your discussion, particularly when it is simply about resolving technical problems, does not need to be shared with participants – and so keeping it low-key and private is generally the most useful option.

CASE STUDY:

Clear your room of stick insects, pregnant cats or any noisy pets

Noisy pets really are the metaphorical 'banana skin' on which many virtual facilitators slip up at times, if they are working from home at least. And like banana skins, they are possible to avoid, and should be picked up and put out of the way so that they can't affect your session. We have worked with a colleague who ran virtual sessions from a room which also housed a glass cage full of stick insects – his son's favourite pets. The fact that he chose this room was largely due to it being the only private room in his house, rather than the presence of the insects being a positive inspiration to him. And although the sticky creatures didn't actually make a noise, the facilitator always seemed to fear they would do (eating leaves too loudly, perhaps?) or worse – climb out of the cage. He was not an insect lover, and these fears cramped his usually relaxed and confident style more than a little.

Sometimes shutting the door is the only option for pets that like to get up close and personal. Another colleague was running a meeting on Webex from home when her pregnant cat chose that very moment to climb onto her lap and give birth, with all the noise and upheaval one can imagine that event induces.

What to do? The facilitator coped, with remarkable aplomb, by announcing some 'background disturbance' and informing participants she would pop herself on mute for a short while. She asked the producer to provide a filler activity she had lined up with a case study and whiteboard. Clearly the cat was not planning to fit around the agenda of the session, so she quietly phoned her neighbour and asked her for some cat-sitting support until she had finished running the session. Ten out of ten for inventiveness and composure, and for those readers who are worried about the cat – she was fine (and so were her kittens).

Numerous other facilitators we know have dogs who, left unsupervised, may bark at embarrassing moments. Keeping the dog out of the way really is the only option. Unless you have the kind of perfectly-trained dog that knows you are running a virtual session, never barks, and will even go to the kitchen and bring you a cup of tea and a biscuit if you wish. I don't know if that dog exists, but I certainly don't own it.

Manage the space immediately around you.

For many people, one of the beauties of working virtually is that you can be polished and professional without needing to hire a fancy meeting room or wear a smart suit. Which is why so many virtual trainers and coaches work from the comfort and privacy of their own home, sometimes in their pyjamas, if they feel like it.

This is pretty liberating, and also often helps us to feel relaxed and at ease – after all we are 'in our own space'. However, there are certain points that still need to be managed – ignore them at your peril!

In the face to face training room, it goes without saying that any experienced trainer will ensure s/he has undertaken the room 'set up' properly, checked the audio-visual equipment, posted the script (if necessary) somewhere visible in case s/he loses the flow of the session or over-runs on time and needs to make adjustments. Usually, in the face to face classroom or meeting room, we have a checklist of points that will be gone through to make sure everything is ready and in place when we need it.

Setting up the space around you is perhaps even more important when you are working virtually, whether you are working 'visibly', with webcam, or not. Why? Everything that can make a noise, loudly, unexpectedly, distractingly, when you least need it – will do so. Unless, of course, you remove it from your desk so that you cannot touch, trigger or knock it on the floor, or break it.

And in virtual space, when working without visual connection through webcam – unwanted noise takes on a power and presence of its own. Make sure you control it. Here are some practical points which we tend to forget, especially when under pressure.

PRACTICAL TIPS
....

- **Shut the door** of the room you are working in. You do not want to be interrupted – and of course you will have already followed the tip from our earlier chapter on making sure a sign is clearly displayed letting people know you are running a virtual session and cannot be disturbed until it is over.

- **Clear your desk** of clutter so that you have only the absolute essentials you will need in your session. These might include pen, paper, script, watch, list of participant names and contact details/phone numbers, a glass of water and (if required) your reading glasses. Nothing else is needed. Nothing. OK, a bar of chocolate if you really, really must – but see our point below about eating when on microphone.

- **Switch your mobile phone off**, or (if you are using it to communicate with your producer or participants) at least mute it so that you can see it, but not hear it ring, and pick up texts from the producer, if that's how you've agreed you will communicate. Similarly, check the room for any electronic devices you may have overlooked (we include alarm clocks here) that are liable to notify you of their presence when you least need them to.

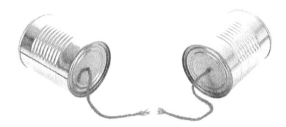

- **Do not drink or eat anything** when wearing a headset with a microphone on – unless you have pushed the mic well away from your mouth first. It's astonishing how good those little mics are at picking up a loud slurp or munch from a hungry facilitator. (NB Webcams are also good at picking up these noises, and will then usually – if your webcam is turned on – visually highlight the person who is making the noise even if they are just having a sneaky sandwich or tea break behind the scenes. Please, please don't make this mistake – too many others have done so before you.)

- **Note-taking:** If you are planning to take notes on your computer when running a session (perhaps to write comments on a slide or whiteboard) – **check whether you have a noisy keyboard or not**. It is astonishing how in some sessions someone who considers themselves to be typing lightly is making an extraordinarily loud thumping noise which all participants are aware of, except the typist himself.

- An experienced producer friend with a noisy keyboard likes to put a cushion underneath it, which seems to work wonders (you may need to raise your chair a bit so as to match the increased height of the computer keyboard). Others prefer to use a wooden desk to a metal or glass one. Whatever you decide, this is a point to be aware of and take care of in advance.

- Our general rule here would be that when you are taking notes as a facilitator on a group discussion – for example, on whiteboard or slide, for the whole group to see – of course you have no choice but to use your computer keyboard to do so. When you are making a quiet note for yourself on something that is only for you and does NOT need to be shared with others in the group, we prefer to use pen and paper. Old-fashioned, but still effective, and it has the benefit of not disturbing the rest of the group with noisy typing.

- **Use a 'running order' style script as a reference guide only.** We commented in **Chapter Three** about the value of having a printed script to hand, and we always advocate the use of a script so that you can structure your session to the time available. A sample script is included in the **Resources** section under 3.1. It also enables you (and your producer) to be completely familiar with the order of slides you wish to show, and with the other activities that will be running in-session. Remember that having a script does not mean that you have to stick slavishly to it (see our further comments below on balancing flexibility and structure). It just means that you can keep to time effectively and know what you have to hand as and when you need it.

And finally – a word of warning. When people present in virtual space for the first time, they may often feel a little nervous and unsure of themselves. Quite often in that situation a script feels like a prop, something we can rely on entirely to carry us through. But we strongly advise that you ALWAYS resist the temptation to over-prepare with a word-for-word script which you read out.

Reading from a script never works, for a whole variety of reasons. The first is that your voice will come out sounding mechanical, lifeless and boring. A second reason is that you may lose your place in the script, and then find it far harder to find your way back into the flow of the session. A third is that if you are focusing on a script, you are not focusing on what is happening for your participants – by looking in the Chatbox, if there is one, or at the whiteboard for written comments, or in the Q&A feature for questions – and any other kinds of interaction that may be taking place.

Essentially, a script is really only just a series of headings and activities to work to , not a word-by-word speech to follow. So placing the script in front of you so that you can glance at it when you need to, certainly helps – it's there when you need it. It also means you avoid turning your head to read a script on a table beside you, which can affect your voice quality to a surprising extent. People can hear that you have turned away from the computer and your voice will lose emphasis, and you may sound disengaged.

- **Also use a 'slide script'** to show the visual flow of your session. Some facilitators also like to have handy a printed slide script, showing thumbnail slides at around 6 to 9 to a page, all numbered. Still others combine the slide script with the running order script so they have the visual script with slides, timings and activities all listed together. This is all about personal preference, but having a printed slide script simply reminds you of the visual flow of the session, and the slides that will be coming up.

Just as importantly, a slide script helps you to move between slides rapidly without getting lost – should this need arise – because you will see the order the slides appear in, and can find your way via the numbering system to the slide you want quickly and without fuss. There's nothing worse than inflicting your entire set of slides on unsuspecting participants as you go through them one at a time – simply because you cannot find that one pesky slide you were hoping to locate in a hurry. That kind of clumsiness is not only a timewaster; it also strips the session of any element of mystery and anticipation, both of which are good for engagement.

Prepare yourself physically to facilitate.

It really helps if you are sitting somewhere comfortably with your body upright but relaxed, your lungs open, your feet planted firmly on the ground, your head facing forward rather than down.

Having an open, strong body posture without being slumped or overly rigid not only helps you breathe better and feel more calm, it also helps your voice to sound confident, and – no surprise here – you are then more likely to end up feeling confident. We also notice that working to a desktop – or at least a laptop with a screen at eye level – is very helpful, because your head is up and so, as a result, is your voice. Looking down at the screen means your head will be slightly dipped, and this can lower the volume and generally compress your vocal chords, and therefore the impact of your voice. It really is surprising what a significant positive difference these small adjustments can make.

Some facilitators work with a Bluetooth headset, enabling them to move freely and not be wired to the computer. At present, these wifi headsets still present some audio setbacks at times, so we prefer to be connected to the computer on a plug-in headset, even with the constraint that this restricts free movement around the room. As time goes on, however, these current drawbacks to facilitating 'on the move' via a wifi headset are likely to disappear as technology improves continuously.

And if now you are thinking – well, nothing too surprising in this list of responsibilities – you are right. Getting ready for the session is practical common-sense, and there is nothing here that cannot be acquired with determination, passion and practice. That word again …

PRACTISE …PRACTISE …PRACTISE

- Practising and gaining experience on your platform of choice in your own time – alone, or with a producer or supportive friend – is not only desirable, it is particularly easy these days because basic (free) versions of many software platforms are widely available, and many of the basic set-ups also have some of the most commonly used tools and features that you access through the more expensive versions.

- **Meet yourself in cyber space.** For those who do not wish to impose too much on the aforementioned 'supportive friend', think about joining yourself for a meeting in cyber space. Futuristic as this may sound, it just means that if you use two computers, you can join the session on one computer as the host/presenter, and on the other as an attendee. This enables you to see what the participant sees when you are presenter, and to practise activities like setting up breakout rooms, running polls, and so on – both running them, and participating in them, at the same time..

(You may even find that you draw yourself into an engaging debate, or even a full-scale argument, on a topic of interest. Just try and do this privately, in case a well-wisher overhears you arguing with yourself and does not understand that there is some kind of method in your madness.)

Seven skills that virtual facilitators need – or 'flying by the seat of your pants' in cyber space?

A word before we go further. This is not an onerous list, and again we could probably make that title '20 skills' or even '50…' if we thought hard enough about it. But if seven dwarfs were good enough for Snow White, seven skills are good enough for us. And these are the ones that really stand out to us as top of the list. They are based not only on what we've learned over the years, but also what students tell us they found were most important when they first began putting themselves out there in cyber space as virtual facilitators.

Skill Number One: Keep calm and carry on

Let's face it, for many of us there are numerous times in our lives when we start a sentence without knowing how we will finish it. Being a virtual facilitator can be a bit like that. Even while we are speaking, new things are happening, there are competing demands for our attention, and there may be many things to keep an eye on all at once. And while you can't ignore them, once you become distracted by them, you might lose the point of what you were talking about in the first place.

The point is, none of that matters if you suggest that it doesn't. Your ability to stay calm and relaxed (and to sound it, and show it) is really everything.

Keeping calm and avoiding panic – rushing the pace, sounding uncomfortable, jumping awkwardly through the slide deck or whiteboards as you try to find what you want – this is evidently a key skill for budding virtual facilitators, as for more experienced ones. Losing your cool and your control of the session will neither help your participants to feel confident that you can guide them through it, nor help you generally keep energy high, if you need to.

Working virtually, even backed by an excellent producer, you will notice that you are looking at, and dealing with, a whole range of things at any one time. You may be running a slide presentation and inviting comments from your group as you do that; whilst trying to reply to each remark individually and link it with your theme. At the same time you may be looking in the Chatbox and noticing that one person is complaining of background noise and wants you to do something about it. Your producer may be calling you on your mobile – or sending an instant text – to explain that she needs to sort out a participant who is having trouble joining.

All these communications are coming to you at the same time, and you still need to be able to 'field' them all calmly, prioritise, and keep the flow of the session.

We suggest that composure is all, and the ability to improvise when necessary. Here are some practical tips to achieve that.

PRACTICAL TIPS

- **Take time before the session starts to breathe, calm down and feel properly 'grounded' physically and mentally.** This is helpful preparation for dealing with an action-packed and unpredictable session. And, even if all goes absolutely smoothly (this does happen sometimes, believe us) the process of composing yourself and quietly preparing in advance in this way can only help you sound as polished, professional and engaging as you would like to be.

- The technical back-up of **a reliable producer** is another theme we've mentioned several times already. It is not a luxury; in many cases (especially when working with bigger groups) it is an essential. Enough said.

- **Share the dilemma and let people know what you are doing about it.**
  If something causes a problem – perhaps your slides disappear, or your
  wireless headset runs out of charge – this is not the time to 'make a big
  production' out of the issue, clearly. But it is essential to let your producer
  know, and via him or her, your participants that something has gone wrong
  and you can quickly remedy it. Trying to conceal problems that will affect
  the whole group in a virtual session simply doesn't work. If you are no longer
  audible, but do not explain why, or if you appear to have left the meeting,
  but without saying goodbye – your producer and your participants may fear
  a major disaster rather than a small, resolvable 'glitch'. And their concerns
  may get in the way of them paying attention to the rest of the session.

- In general, it is much better to be open about a problem that affects more
  than, say, two people in a group. Participants will be reassured to know what
  the difficulty is and that you or the producer are taking care of it. And what
  are they doing while you resolve the problem and (if necessary) get the
  session back on track? They are not getting bored, instead they are engaging
  in something you devised earlier, because you …

- As hot tips goes, this may be one of the hottest. If for any reason you,
  the facilitator, are obliged to leave the session to remedy a problem you
  are facing, or put yourself on 'mute' for a short while, you need to have
  something to fill that gap. Unplanned silence with nothing to do is the virtual
  facilitator's ultimate nightmare. In virtual space, it is always a good idea to
  have a 'filler' activity or 'Plan B' up your sleeve, which you discuss with the
  producer beforehand so that s/he can run it for you if the need arises.

  What might the filler activity be? A simple example is having a topic for
  discussion on a slide, and asking participants to share their views, and note
  them on a whiteboard. The topic for discussion should clearly relate to
  the agenda of the session, or this can seem random indeed. And, if you do
  include a 'filler' like this, you will need to make sure you debrief it properly,
  or people may feel they have wasted their time.

Filler Activity: 'I think I can feel a song coming on ....'

Another slightly more unusual idea offered by one of our producers when the facilitator had to leave and rejoin the session unexpectedly due to audio challenges, was to arrange a 'round' – or singing, one after the other, a song where each line harmonises with the one after it. I'm not certain if the song ('Frère Jacques') itself was particularly instructive, but the activity was very warmly received, encouraging excellent listening skills in virtual space, as well as the confidence to sing alone with a bunch of invisible strangers. Possibly not for the faint-hearted, or in a more formal training session – but still, worth considering perhaps?

- Things sometimes go wrong. Get used to it. And above all, don't panic. As one of our training slides puts it (with a certain amount of irony): 'When all else fails, shout 'Help' and wave your arms about'. But we really don't recommend this as a strategy for virtual facilitation success, not only because it may seem unprofessional, but also because it undoubtedly **won't** help.

Skill Number Two: Engage your Ears

This one speaks for itself. Without expert listening skills, your ability to build relationships and tailor content to suit your participants' needs in virtual sessions is pretty much reduced to zero. You will have a limited idea of what your participants make of your session and, if they feel you are not listening to their responses and comments, are likely to quickly lose interest and stop listening to you in return.

An expert listener, on the other hand, can cope with individual challenges, show empathy and warmth, suggest answers to all kinds of questions, and really succeed in helping attendees at your sessions feel involved, valued and understood. Just as important, you will show that you are listening, something which really matters in any kind of virtual session, but particularly when participants and facilitator cannot see each other.

Much is written about 'expert' or active listening, and in many ways it might seem like such an 'old topic' to some trainers and coaches that the temptation is to just assume that what we do when working face to face will be enough in virtual space. However, there are certain ways of showing your listening skills when working virtually that have a particularly positive impact. Here are some practical suggestions we have found effective.

PRACTICAL TIPS

- Be clear from the start that you are aiming for a conversation, not a one-way presentation (if such is the case) and invite people to interact throughout your session

- Be as inclusive as possible, given the timeframe of your session, and make clear in any particular activity whether you are going to invite comments from everyone in turn, or just two or three quick responses. This way, people know what to expect and won't feel overlooked.

- By keeping a list of the names of participants near you in the session, you can make sure that you have included everyone in a Check In exercise, or some other activity that involves a response from each person

- When you are running a debrief of a particular activity, and hearing comments from everyone in the group, engage – even briefly – with each comment that is made, and acknowledge it. When people can't see you and you don't comment on what they've said, it can feel like being ignored – or they may not even know if you've heard them

- **Always** thank people for their comments.

We also say more about 'Listening' in describing our 'VELVET' model for developing your style as a facilitator below.

Skill Number Three: Actively invite feedback

In the face to face training room, there is usually an activity at the end of the programme where people are invited to give feedback via an evaluation form, or in some other way. We do the same in our virtual sessions, for the usual reason that it helps us to know where we've succeeded, and what we need to fine-tune for another occasion.

However, giving and receiving feedback as a virtual facilitator is a key skill that you will find yourself using throughout your sessions, not just at the end. Of course we do not mean by this that you should always be anxiously checking whether you, as facilitator, are 'doing OK' – or not.

We do mean that, in the absence of visual clues and the kind of physical connection you have in the face to face classroom, asking people to let you know what they are finding helpful and interesting, or less so, is very important as a means to keep engagement and energy high, and to adjust the flow of the session if necessary.

We generally invite people to do this at least twice in any two hour session. It doesn't have to be a long conversation. Here are some ways of inviting feedback in your virtual sessions.

PRACTICAL TIPS

- Use a tool such as the **'Engagement Barometer'**. This is a slide which invites people to write on the slide what the 'highs' and 'lows' of the session have been for them, and discuss them. An effective activity towards the end of the session.

HIGHS   LOWS

- Invite people to respond to activities by using the **'emoticons' palette or feedback tools** that are available on many meetings platforms currently. Indeed, once they know they are there, they will probably use them anyway, whether you invite them or not! While the range is still not particularly extensive, you can see at a quick glance whether people are using the (hopefully) 'big smile, loving it' face. If they're using the 'falling asleep' or 'confused expression', you're going to have to do something about it.

- One trainer we have been particularly struck by in the past – he worked face to face, but there's no reason why this shouldn't work in a virtual group – used to ask his students at regular intervals for **'questions, comments, sarcastic remarks?'** It may be that you need to know your group a little before you can ask for the 'sarcastic remarks', and they need to understand your sense of humour. However, in general asking for reflections and comments throughout a session is an excellent way to check engagement.

But you will need to allow time for this kind of spontaneous feedback in your session plan.

- Listen to the feedback you receive, ask clarifying questions about it if necessary, thank people for it, and (if you agree with it) act upon it.

- Always end a 'one-off' training session, or longer training or coaching programme, with an evaluation form. You can set this up online and invite people to complete and submit it while you still have them in session with you. Sending on by email later usually doesn't work – get those invaluable commentaries and ratings immediately, before people leave and forget all about it.

A quick point about giving feedback, which is of course another skill you may wish to use regularly in your training, coaching and meetings delivery. This is as valuable to participants meeting across distance as it is to people meeting in the same room, and it is also a way to maintain engagement. You will find a tool we find consider particularly useful in giving feedback listed in the *Resources* section of this book.

Skill Number Four: Multi-task!

There really is no way around it. At any one point in a virtual meeting, training or coaching session you may be doing up to five things at once (random figure, but you get the idea). At the start of a session, you may be welcoming participants, making conversation with them, checking your chat space, uploading your slides, and ensuring that everyone's audio is up to scratch (especially if you have ignored our previous advice, and do not have a producer to help you!)

And this sort of full-on activity is likely to continue throughout the session or meeting.

Even if someone else is presenting on a topic and you can 'sit back' a little – you most definitely cannot entirely 'switch off'. If technical challenges or questions arise, you need to be ready to manage them, and to give feedback to the person who is presenting, if required.

When you add to that the additional need to sound friendly, composed and in control – it's no small matter for most of us to achieve that consistently, and perhaps particularly tough for facilitators or trainers who prefer to do one thing at a time.

While multi-tasking is just something you will have to get used to (and in these days of hectic schedules and conflicting time pressures you may very well be already more than used to it) – practice again makes perfect.

Skill Number Five: Combine flexibility AND structure

You've probably guessed this by now, but over time you will find that you barely glance at your script; it is just there to reassure you that you are on track as and when you need that reassurance. As the old saying has it – the rules are made to be broken, and a script is made to be ignored when you feel the occasion allows – whether because it doesn't quite match what participants hope for at that moment, or because questions come up that need to be addressed.

But it is hard to depart from the script and improvise if you do not have a script in the first place. Flexibility only works, paradoxically, if you have planned for it – otherwise you are looking at chaos. And none of us need that.

One of the most important challenges you will need to face as a virtual facilitator is that of balancing the need to get on with the task at hand (following the structure you have designed already) with allowing 'spontaneity', in the form of deviations and interruptions from people who are particularly interested in going into one topic in more depth, or even going 'off piste' altogether with something entirely different.

There really is no single way to get this balance right. It depends on several factors – your style and preferences as a facilitator; the expectations and needs of your client; the 'chemistry' of the group itself, what group members enjoy and how well they get on together.

All that said, here are a few tips for achieving a suitable balance.

PRACTICAL TIPS

- **Avoid overstructuring.** Running a session that is so tightly structured that there is no room AT ALL for deviation – for example, when people have questions and comments that will take time to answer – is a very big mistake. Why? Because you as facilitator will have to ignore the opportunities that arise to have an engaging discussion, or go into a particular point in slightly more depth. The need to keep to your agenda in these circumstances takes over to such an extent that you may find you simply 'disconnect' from your participants' needs, in order to stick to the plan and do what you set out to do.

- **Allow some time for flexibility in your approach.** There is no hard and fast rule about this, but we prefer to allow up to 15 minutes of 'flexibility time' in a 2 hour virtual session – meaning time when you might decide to 'go with the flow' and see what emerges. In any case, as we discuss in our next point, you will find that everything takes longer than you expect in virtual space and so some 'spare' time is always helpful as you may need it to get through the session's structure in any case.

- **Keep your objectives in mind at all times** and refer to them occasionally. Extreme flexibility – entirely ignoring the 'plan' for the meeting or session and allowing participants' needs to dominate the flow without any consideration of intended outcomes – may seem like a good idea at the time, but ultimately runs the risk of confusing and disappointing people. Of course as face to face trainers we would always keep this in mind – unless the training session or meeting is all about 'free flowing creativity' with no set agenda, that is.

- **Honour participants who need focus and a clear-cut process.** Working virtually, you meet all kinds of people. Some of whom are happy to be playful and go with the flow from the beginning of your session, others who need a bit of hand-holding and sense of purpose. Working virtually can be an exhilarating experience at first for many, with plenty of tools to discover and opportunities to explore. This is exciting, and it can also be confusing. In many ways, the structure, objectives or 'backbone' of a session is there to provide comfort and reassure that the virtual meeting has focus, for those people who need that, and very many will.

- **Create playful opportunities for playful participants.** If you have very imaginative, high energy participants who are constantly fired up by trying something different, you need to allow some specified 'playtime' for exploration. However, be careful about setting limits here. In reality, 100% flexibility in a virtual session usually means that you have no prepared materials, and that you need those very imaginative and energised participants to tell you what they want. If they do not know, and you have nothing up your sleeve, you are all likely to be looking at a blank screen for a minute or two, at least. So while there are many opportunities in virtual meetings to fire your participants' interest spontaneously, you are still likely to need something onside to achieve this, via visual stimuli and specific suggestions for activities to undertake together.

Skill Number Six: Managing time under pressure

There is a simple rule here. Everything takes longer than you think in virtual space. You can probably expect to carry out one activity every 15 minutes, if you want to have some discussion about it, and allow time for questions. If you are doing something which needs a bit of set-up time, such as running breakout sessions, 15 minutes will not be enough.

Most people starting out as virtual facilitators (the authors and some of our former students included) devise a script for their first session or so which allows no room for flexibility, and where every second is accounted for. Invariably, they run out of time and realise halfway through their sessions that they are just going to have to think again, and lose some activities, perhaps choosing to focus on one in depth, and allow time to talk about it.

In some ways, managing time is a skill which brings together many of the other required abilities of a virtual facilitator – listening, creativity, resilience, keeping calm, multi-tasking, balancing structure and flexibility – and so on.

Here are some ideas that can help you stay on track with time in your session.

PRACTICAL TIPS
....

- Keep a watch handy, or at least keep an eye on the clock on your computer.

- Be clear with participants how much time they have for any activity, and that you may need to interrupt them if time runs short. This usually means that they will actively support you in keeping to time, rather than feeling annoyed at being 'cut short' in an activity unexpectedly.

- Always assume less is more. In a two-hour session, expect to be able to cover four different activities at the most (depending to some extent on what they are, and how engaged the group is, naturally). Do not have a script so tightly planned that there is no room for error or deviation.

- Delegate time management to your producer or a participant, if you find it difficult to be assertive with keeping to time.

- Some facilitators prefer to simply show a slide with a clock on it, to indicate that time is up, rather than always have to do so vocally. It has even been known for the facilitator to write on a presenter's slide: 'Time is up now' – in order not to interrupt. Other facilitators, on the other hand, quite enjoy the rigour of abruptly stopping a conversation that has run over time. It's 'horses for courses', and depends on your style, and what your group prefers, of course.

Always include a 5 minute break in a 2 hour session. You will find people return with more energy and so you can make maximum use of the time available in the second half of your session.

- Do not try and do synchronously – in session – what you can do asynchronously – out of session. If people ask a lot of questions, be clear how many you can address on the spot. In an ongoing programme or one-off session, you might make a note of the outstanding questions and offer to respond to them in writing once the session has closed, and circulate to other participants if the answers are generally useful to all.

- **Keep the time focused** in your live sessions on discussion and activity – not on replying in depth to one participant's topic of interest. If you can answer a question briefly and informatively, do. If it needs more time, and is not relevant to the whole group, you may need to manage it offline, or ask the person to remain behind at the end of the session when you will be able to talk in more depth.

Finally, and much more briefly, a last point is to …

Skill Number Seven: Be ready to have fun and enjoy yourself …
There is little more we can say on this point. It is not something you can plan for, but it will happen. Almost any topic of discussion can be enjoyable if you take the time to get to know the group engaged with it, and to find interesting and innovative ways to trigger reflection and debate. Getting to know each person in the group a little better, to understand more about them than when you started the session – well, that is very often fun, inspiring, and energising.

So while we cannot instruct you to have fun and enjoy all your sessions, we hope that will happen in most of them – naturally, and as you continue to practise and polish your skills. Because there is so much fun and enjoyment to be had out there, in the playground of the virtual classroom.

Developing your 'style' in virtual space

Now you know more about the role, responsibilities and skills of an effective and engaging virtual facilitator, you may want to think about what you personally, with your own strengths, preferences and challenges bring to that role, and the impact you specifically want to have on others when running virtual meetings and events.

CASE STUDY:

Style 'snapshots' in virtual sessions

In one of our training programmes we focus specifically on gaining skills in virtual facilitation. With a recent group of learners in that programme we invited people about half way through the programme to think about this question of their own individual 'style' as a facilitator, and to prepare and present a slide about it to the rest of the group. The brief was simple: use images and a few limited words to suggest the kind of mood you wish to create in your sessions, and how you wish people to perceive you. Also include a 'saying' or 'mantra' that briefly sums up the impact you want to make on people in general.

The slides turned out to be a genuine revelation. They were highly visual in most cases – relying on symbols and images to suggest ideas rather than words, to suggest a certain mood, or 'flavour' to the sessions. Impressions shared were rich with metaphor and variety, ranging from 'take people safely beyond their comfort zone into a new journey' through ideas like 'provide a safety net and solid ground for exploration in cyber space', to 'have a laugh or two, to play and help people have fun while learning new things'.

Here is just one of the slides prepared for that session, from a woman who had significant experience in delivering sessions virtually, but had never appreciated before the possibilities of developing connections and relationships with her clients in live sessions through visual stimuli in slides, video and other tools.

Having worked together for five weeks already by then, people commented on how they had already noticed the differences in style of delivery among their group of 9 people. Following these comments, we interviewed as many of this group, and others, as possible to find out what participants thought really stood out for them in working out what made the difference between individual styles and approaches among facilitators.

To these general themes we added our own insights, and condensed them into a memorable acronym. We hope the six general headings of the VELVET model shared here will resonate for you as you develop your style further, building strengths and tackling challenges along the way.

'VELVET': Six aspects of your virtual facilitation style

So – what about you? What kind of impact do you wish to make on others as a virtual facilitator? If you were asked to summarise your hoped-for style in one or two images, what might they be? If you had to provide a saying or phrase that summarises the way you would like to be perceived by your participants, what words would you use?

In this next section, we invite you to consider each of the six aspects of 'style' we discuss, and think about how you prefer to work. What challenges lie in this particularly topic for you? What are the strengths you already perceive? What would you like to do differently, less and more of? In considering these questions, we hope you will also find some practical tips to help you with particular goals that you may set yourself.

V is for Virtual Etiquette – communication 'rules' and establishing the mood
Virtual Etiquette – also called 'Netiquette' – is referred to several times in this book, and there is a fuller description of it in ***Chapter Four***. The old-fashioned word 'Etiquette' refers of course to the 'rules of behaviour' used in any given situation, which are often implicit rather than expressed. This might mean, for example the appropriate 'etiquette' regarding – for example – how to meet and greet others in a social situation, how to behave while in the company of your boss, how to eat in polite company – these are all codes of behaviour which are determined partly by culture, partly according to individual preference, and which, if disregarded or ignored, can be surprisingly detrimental to one's career or relationships.

In virtual space, knowing 'the rules' of communication in a meeting or training session is just as important, and this may mean considering some aspects of communication in far more detail than we would ever imagine doing in face to face contact. Of course, a face to face conversation is actually a great deal more complicated (and heavily contextualised) than it may appear on the surface. We are so used to communicating in this way that we hardly notice how much each person does to make eye contact, or try to read the non-verbal gestures and facial expression of the other, and connect with him or her in a meaningful way.

Mostly, these activities are instinctive, and we barely notice we are doing them. The rules are rarely expressed, and on most occasions we intuitively know how to follow them, unless (for example) we are working with strangers from a culture we know little about.

In cyber space, the non-verbal messages are largely lacking, or at least greatly reduced, even with webcam available. So while in a face to face conversation it would seem ludicrous – not to say bizarre – to ask a trainer, or colleague: 'How would you like me to interrupt you, when I disagree or have a question?', in a virtual session it is often imperative to establish this basic conversational rule.

Here are some questions which it is usually helpful for facilitators to ask themselves at the start of the session, particularly if it's the first time you are facilitating, but even if it's not. Some of them may seem 'micro' and trivial at first glance, but not bothering to address them may well cause confusion later. Knowing what you as facilitator want and expect regarding the 'small rules' of communication in your session makes life clearer and more comfortable for everyone in your virtual session. Just as importantly, it is these small, apparently 'minor' rules which help to establish the mood and atmosphere of your session or meeting.

- Firstly, do we want participants to remain audible for the entire session – in other words, not to be placed on 'mute' unless there is disturbing background noise. This is of course the facilitator's choice. But – well folks, you know what the authors of this book believe creates the best connection, don't you? (Clue: Muting everyone is not known for its effectiveness in building relationships and creating engagement.)

- Silence tends to weigh more heavily when we cannot see the people we are talking to – what do we want participants to do when there is extended silence, if anything?

- What might we consider doing if several seconds silence comes unexpectedly (ie not following a reflective exercise) and we want to know what is happening?

- How do we want participants to interrupt us during the session, if at all? Should we invite them to just 'jump in' aloud, or do (for example) by writing on the slide, in chatspace – and so forth?

- What do we want our attendees to do if they wish to ask a question? Speak up? Write in chat space, or in the Q&A space? Wait until questions are invited? Email us?

- What kind of 'mood' or 'tone do we want the conversation to have? Relaxed? Spontaneous? Formal? Structured? Entertaining? Serious? Inspiring? Reflective?

- Is it OK for participants to 'chat' to others behind the scenes via Chatbox, for example, so that the facilitator is not included in the conversation?

- How much support do we want to offer participants if they experience a technical problem, and how? Will we do this through a producer, and if so how will we communicate with him/her? Or, if contacting participants direct, will we do so directly by phone, or via email or a platform like Skype? All these minor questions are worth considering in advance, before the need arises. It saves a lot of time to clarify this, and everyone needs to be clear what level of support they can expect.

- If a participant wants to leave the session, should s/he say goodbye? And supposing s/he just wants to disappear for a minute or two for a comfort break, or to make a coffee – should s/he bother telling people? Should s/he put herself on mute to keep background noise down for the rest of the participants?

You might find it helpful to consider this list above – and other questions that come to mind when thinking about the 'rules of communication' that support your session. And of course we are not all likely to want the same things, or give the same answers to these questions. Virtual etiquette, to this extent, is not just about 'ways to behave', but also about values – the kind of atmosphere you seek to establish in cyber space, how you want your participants to feel when working with you live online.

Whatever your own 'virtual etiquette', it is a good idea to do the following in any 'one-off' session or when starting a programme with a new group.

PRACTICAL TIP

- Discussing and **clarifying** 'the rules' at the start is very helpful, so people know what to expect and how to contribute. Some groups may wish to discuss and negotiate their own 'team communication rules' and this can be both a useful exercise and a powerful bonding activity for a new group or team. This kind of open discussion with a team or group helps to build confidence, trust, and a safe space for a productive, explorative dialogue.

CASE STUDY:

Headset or phone? Not such a small consideration ...

Sometimes the rules of virtual etiquette can include apparent niceties such as whether participants join a session via telephone or VOIP, (Voice Over Internet Protocol) with a headset. A great many companies favour VOIP these days since many platforms provide excellent audio facilities – following the kind of basic guidelines we set out in this book – for individual access with a headset.

What's important is to **be consistent** in what you tell people in the joining instructions. One of our alumni, Sue, tells us about a virtual team coaching session she joined, run by a company who had invited everyone to make use of a headset and join the meeting by VOIP. When she joined it turned out that she was one of only two people (in a group of 18) who

Continued ...

Continued from page 100

was using a headset, and was put on 'mute' straightaway by the trainer. When she sent him a message to ask why, the trainer replied aloud that the company didn't favour using headsets because the audio is 'too sensitive' and allows all kinds of background noise to be picked up. Feeling 'different' and a bit cut off from the group (since all those who joined by phone were not muted), Sue decided she did not like the confusingly mixed message the company had put out, and was put off attending any further coaching sessions.

E is for Emotional Connection and Energy

Experience shows that, when communicating virtually, many clients leap abruptly to the topic or task they wish to explore without any friendly preliminaries. The strange thing is that this would rarely happen in face to face meetings, unless you are working with some particularly emotionally detached people (or robots – although even they can be programmed to ask caring questions and enquire about your family's wellbeing). Starting a meeting without even a friendly 'how are you?' or 'how are things going?' would be deemed rude in some cultures, and in many others there would be an expectation that the 'social preliminaries' might extend for quite some time, in order for people to feel engaged and comfortable.

Why does this often not happen when we work virtually? It's as though communicating via the Internet somehow causes people to forget that we are human beings and prompts us to behave (in the extreme, at least) like high-functioning machines, with a job to do, but no feelings. Nerves and apprehension, for example, can increase the likelihood of a more formal and distant delivery, because people can hide behind the structure and PowerPoint presentation they have designed without having to engage with their audience.

At other times, the desire to cover as much ground as possible in a short time is the spur that leads facilitators and presenters to get very 'task-oriented' right from the start of their session, without taking any time to establish and 'warm up' the relationship with the group. A further factor is that we have become used to passive webinar-style delivery from facilitators, whereby attendees can often become a passive audience without a voice, and the fact of communicating via technology often 'freezes people up' a bit, and prompts them to behave more formally than usual.

What is the effect of all this? When people focus entirely on the task, they may forget to treat each other like human beings. This, one might argue, happens to a certain extent even when working face to face, when, say, project teams get together under severe time pressure and panic about getting things done to tight deadlines. However, in virtual space, where we are often invisible and unable to make physical contact, it is even more of a risk.

When meeting in person, we can smile, shake hands, make eye contact and chat. In virtual space, we may be looking at a blank computer screen. Focusing on building relationships before going to the task at hand reminds the facilitator (and hopefully everyone in the group) that we are real, live, attentively listening human beings capable of empathic communication.

Time and again, we have had feedback from our students that they had never realised how possible it is when communicating live in virtual sessions to get to know and like people, even to care about them – to become, in other words, emotionally engaged with them to a greater or lesser extent.

While that may not be the 'topline' requirement of every training or coaching programme, or project team meeting, there is ample research to show that this kind of warm, engaged and collaborative connection between participants really does help people work with commitment and mutual support more effectively, and achieve their goals more efficiently against time constraints (Cune, Fogelberg, 2011). It also makes the virtual sessions much more interesting, because where there is emotional connection, there is usually increased energy and engagement, as well as better recall of key learning points, according to neuroscientists (op. cit Campbell, Finkelstein, Whitehead, 2009).

So again, back to you. If you train or coach people face to face, how do you seek to establish a supportive relationship and build trust? And how do you plan to do this in virtual sessions?

Here are some ideas to help you achieve emotional connection with attendees in your virtual sessions.

PRACTICAL TIPS

- **A Check In and Check Out**. We've already covered this in earlier chapters. It helps to set the tone for the session, and for each person in the group to understand how the others are feeling, and what their mood is. Of course, it's short – this is not a counselling session. But it is a friendly and emotionally engaged way to get going with the session with openness and increased understanding, and trust.

- Using **video and music** in your sessions often has a powerful emotional pull, sometimes bringing people together around common experiences.

CASE STUDY

In one of our recent training programmes, a participant showed a particularly moving video for doctors communicating with people living with cancer. The video in itself was fairly harrowing material, it is true, and one attendee was in tears after she saw it. However, what came across in the discussion that followed was not so much that the video was hard-hitting emotionally, but that the experience of seeing it, relating it to a personal situation, and then feeling able to discuss that story with a group of engaged and supportive listeners created a strong emotional bond between people in this group.

- Devising **group projects** which involve commitment, and close observation, is an excellent way to encourage people to build relationships and pay special attention to each other. One way we do this in some multi-session programmes is by inviting each participant in a group to observe another, and prepare an appreciative 'graduation' speech for him or her at the end of the programme. We keep quiet about who is preparing a speech for whom, to add an element of surprise (while this is probably not the most thrilling secret in the world, it adds a pleasant note of mystery to the ongoing programme).

THE MUSICAL GRADUATION SPEECH

In one of our recent closing sessions, a particularly dedicated attendee took enormous trouble with the graduation speech she prepared for another participant. She not only researched a little of his professional background via the Internet, but prepared a range of slides with a musical accompaniment, coordinating the animated points on the slide so that they appeared with a particular beat of the accompanying music. The result: an almost 'filmic' speech which really moved the person on the receiving end of it!

Taking this kind of trouble and paying attention to really understand someone in a virtual group can be just as powerful an experience in virtual sessions as in face to face ones.

- Gauge the mood of the group and **vary your style and energy** accordingly. Even if you are a 'high energy' trainer when working face to face, this pacey, upbeat style does not necessarily work with every group in virtual sessions. One of our students, Khalif, typically delivers extremely energetic training sessions face to face with a large group of people, up to 100 or more. In the training room, he is constantly on the move, talking fast and with considerable power to keep things moving. As the topic he usually speaks about is 'high impact presentation', this kind of delivery is entirely suitable in the face to face setting. However, when he recently tried a session virtually, focusing on a very different topic – how to improve your memory as a learner – he fell back on the same kind of full-on, energetic, presentational style. The result was somewhat disastrous – people told him that they had felt 'hurried along', and that they had found his delivery 'aggressive' and 'pushy', with little time to talk and reflect.

  In virtual space, we can use our voice in certain ways to energise and motivate participants in our sessions – and more is said about this below. However, we need to acknowledge that working virtually often requires a somewhat more reflective and conversational delivery than we might use face to face, a different kind of 'energy', if you will. If people are not visible, and we talk 'at' them too forcefully, they may simply feel overwhelmed by us, rather than stimulated to contribute. At the same time, a 'flatter' kind of delivery with a slower pace may work well in one to one coaching or counselling sessions, but could be a little boring when working with virtual project groups or remote teams. Professional context is all.

- **Personalise content where appropriate.** If you are introducing a new topic to your group or team, for example, say something about why it interests you, what you particularly want to explore about it, and share the story about how you first came across the theme. When a participant does this, the personal insights they share engage the interest of others and stimulate them to support the learning process, because they understand more fully why it matters to the person speaking about it. Ideas come to life for everyone when they have an emotional connection with the person sharing them.

- **Be sociable, play, use humour.** A word of caution before we go into this. By 'using humour', we do not (necessarily) mean telling jokes. And of course, what actually constitutes a 'funny joke' varies considerably from one national culture to the next – indeed inappropriate, insensitive use of humour can cause serious offence and damage relationships. Deliberately trying to be funny is not always possible, nor does it always particularly work well in virtual sessions – unless you are a professional comedian, that is (and sometimes not even then).

Nevertheless, this is not an invitation to be 'deadly dull and serious' in your sessions, without any attempt at levity. What we do mean by playfulness and using humour is – not taking yourself so seriously that you can't laugh with your participants, or 'warm the atmosphere' with some light-hearted comments at times when – say – things may go wrong unexpectedly. Warmth, openness, honesty, showing your humanity – these are all excellent ways to achieve emotional connection and energise your virtual colleagues or students.

Two practical ways to achieve a sociable and playful mood in virtual sessions:

- Why not create a virtual **'meeting place' or 'coffee corner'** – one of our favourite ideas – where people can join, check their audio, and have a relaxed chat among themselves while others come online. The kind of talk that comes up in the virtual coffee corner is often different from what is said in the session: the conversation is more friendly, relaxed and perhaps somewhat less guarded. It really is similar to the ways people speak when they come to catch up on the gossip by the coffee machine, or water cooler, at work.

- Or it may be that you **create a 'filler activity'** so that, for example, people joining the session early have something to do before the entire group is present. There are plenty of these activities, and one we particularly like involves showing a slide with a particular café somewhere in the world, supported by 'clues' such as local dishes, traditional dress, and so forth. The first person to guess the location of the café wins …. nothing, usually, except the admiration of the others. Such is life. But even without a tangible reward, people like the competition, and activities like this can create a positive spark of energy at the start of your session.

L is for … Listening with Curiosity

Listening at the deepest level of awareness is a core skill for coaches. But in virtual space, how do clients know we are paying attention, especially if silent and invisible? Even with a webcam, cues such as body movement and facial gestures are often unavailable.

We have already said quite a bit about listening when talking about key skills for virtual facilitators, so in addition to the information and tips already suggested above, here a few more thoughts. Mark Lister makes an important distinction (Lister, 2015) – the difference between 'listening to interrupt' and 'listening to understand'. Listening to interrupt is not really listening at all – it is simply waiting for an opening in the conversation to jump in with our own (possibly conflicting) point of view.

Listening to understand is something else entirely, and it involves, to some extent, putting our own needs on hold until we are certain we have fully understood what has been said, and can offer something useful to connect with it. Listening to understand may involve asking questions about what has been said, summarising what we have heard, reflecting and sharing our feelings and reactions to it, helping the speaker realise they have been heard, and paid attention to.

Listening to understand in virtual space is a deeply empathic activity. By which we mean – it really involves trying to put yourself in the other person's shoes, and (if we may mix metaphors) see the world through his or her eyes, rather than our own interpretations. When working virtually, this kind of listening may show itself in a close attention to the client's words, but it is also likely to involve awareness of his or her nonverbal utterances – coughs, changes of tone, hesitations, pauses—all of which we hear more intensely when physical contact is missing. Asking questions about what we hear can be extremely useful at times: (for example) 'What kind of silence is this?' or 'What is the silence telling us?'

At other times, sharing reflections that indicate our physical presence and connection with what is said is another way to show deep listening across distance (e.g., "When you said that, I felt completely surprised. I found myself closing my eyes to try to imagine it" – and so on).

Again, professional context makes a difference here. If working as a trainer with a large group, such an intense focus on listening deeply to each individual may be neither possible nor desirable. If working one to one as a coach or counsellor, it may be essential.

How deep a listener do you think you are? What are you proud of, what do you need to work on more? If we asked your clients how well they feel you pay attention to their views in virtual sessions, what do you think they would say?

V is for …. Vocal Presence
Anyone who has ever had a long phone conversation with someone and fallen in love with their voice (without having actually seen the person concerned) will know for a fact that the sound of a voice can create all kinds of impressions and assumptions. It is perhaps one of the most potentially beguiling, and at the same time misleading aspects of the impression we make upon others, as those smitten by a truly engaging and seductive voice find to their disappointment when its owner materialises, with a physical appearance that does not quite live up to expectations. (And of course, the reverse applies – we may be utterly charmed by a person's physical beauty, but completely turned off by a voice that sounds silly, high-pitched and petulant, or just plain boring.)

In virtual space, establishing our coaching presence requires a new awareness of the impact of our voice – its ability to bring energy and show connection, understanding, enthusiasm, warmth and concern. Many commentators (Caulat, 2012) state that the power of voice in virtual space is second to none, much more impactful than visual presence, via webcam, for example.

We have described earlier in this chapter how working virtually makes it possible to come across as a smooth professional whilst still wearing our pyjamas, and certainly the liberating possibility of relying entirely on 'vocal presence' rather than physical presence offers a certain freedom to the virtual facilitator. Whether or not we enjoy the option of not having to dress smartly for work, we may be interested to consider the kind of opportunities that using our voice to establish our 'presence' as a facilitator across distance opens up for us.

Before some practical considerations, a quick comment. The voice of the facilitator can sometimes be a real source of reassurance to people who are new to working virtually. If we are taking people through some technological features they haven't tried before – the first time a participant joins a breakout session, or leaves it (for example) can sometimes be a rather anxiety-making moment for some – the facilitator's voice is almost like a guiding pair of hands, showing us where to go.

Using your voice with more emphasis and care in virtual space can often be important. We may need to speak more slowly and use pauses and changes of tone and pace to make distinctions between ideas, for example, to underline uncertainties and open conversational 'doors' to new ways of working. When the facilitator is genuinely interested – excited, even – about what s/he is describing, that passion and interest comes across powerfully to those listening. Working virtually is an excellent opportunity to develop vocal presence in an authentic way.

Marieke de Boer is a trainer and voice coach with whom I work regularly in virtual facilitation sessions. She suggests the following ideas to develop the impact and tone of your voice.

- Be authentic. Using your voice well in virtual space does not have to do with speaking differently, or trying to sound like someone different from yourself. It does have to do with making the most of your natural resonance and pitch.

- Think what kind of tone, or image, you want to create with your 'natural voice'. When we explored this with some of our students, we got answers as varying as: 'I would like to come across as friendly and relaxed as a radio presenter'; 'I want to sound like a storyteller, someone with some excitement to share'; and 'I would like to wake people up with my voice, and fill them with energy', 'I want to sound calm, reassuring, and also authoritative' – and so on.

- Relaxing and warming up your voice before a virtual session might involve having a good stretch, yawning, making sure you are rested and your voice is 'clear' by breathing in and out slowly before you start.

- Marieke speaks about the impact of different vocal tones. A higher voice may energise, and a lower voice can sometimes carry more weight and authority. While there is little we can do about the natural pitch of our voice, we can certainly **vary the pace at which we speak, and give a certain weight and emphasis to particular words.** If we know the mood or 'tone' we wish our voice to convey, we can work with that and develop it, within our own natural range.

When you think about your own voice, and how you wish to 'sound' in virtual space, what are the words and images that come to mind? Is there a particular mood you wish to create? What would you say is the natural 'tone' and impact of your voice, and how might you develop this further?

E is for ..... Engaging Visually

When you join a virtual session or meeting as a participant, what is the first thing you see? Is it a friendly and welcoming visual slide, letting you know that you are in the right place at the right time, with an image that draws you in and puts you in a relaxed mood? Or is it a blank screen with almost nothing on it except some small print showing the meeting time and set up?

Engaging visually with your clients starts from the very beginning of your session. First impressions count and tend to stay with people: the visual impact you make as facilitator – via the content you share, whether or not you are actually visible on webcam – is no different.

But visual presence in virtual space refers to more than how you as facilitator wish to be perceived by the client. Without face-to-face contact, we find that the way we use features of the session – whiteboards, slides, video, and so forth – can offer a significant appeal to participants' imagination, eliciting insights shared via scribbled words or drawn or cut-and-pasted images on the slides and whiteboards some online platforms offer.

In many ways, individual ideas and in-the-moment insights and comments can be shared creatively with much greater ease in virtual sessions than they can be in face to face settings. We actively encourage our participants to write or draw their ideas on slides in a way of working we call **'positive graffiti'** (as mentioned earlier in this chapter). There is no equivalent to this in face to face presentation.

We also use whiteboards regularly for scribbling images as well as words. Since people often 'doodle' – or scribble little images and drawings when listening to someone speak – in the face to face classroom, so why not invite 'mood-doodling' in virtual space? One way this might work is during an open discussion of a particular topic or idea, where participants are invited to draw rather than write their reactions or thoughts to what is being said on a shared whiteboard, for all to see. Again, the 'public space' of the whiteboard or slide in virtual working is a source of considerable group creativity.

You will notice in all these examples we talk about the use of images as well as words. Images are considered to have a particular power in triggering the imagination (Morgan, 1993) and we prefer to focus on images rather than text in our slides as much as possible. Some examples of how you might use slides in similar ways are given below, in our list of practical suggestions for 'visual engagement' with your participants.

PRACTICAL TIPS

- **Take care in creating an appealing 'visual learning space' or 'virtual classroom'.** The 'space' that any participant finds him or herself in on joining the session is entirely within your control as virtual facilitator. You may actually be sitting in a cramped study bedroom at home surrounded by unwashed coffee cups to deliver your session (we've all been there, we feel your pain), but in 'virtual space' or the mind's eye, you could be anywhere. With creative slides and use of other features, you can create the sensation of running the session from a tropical beach, the top of a mountain at sunrise, or (for those who like a more corporate feel, nevertheless) a smart set of offices with an Executive PA and the latest designer furniture. The mood you create and the imaginative space you set up around you through your content really is a key part of the impact you make as facilitator. That starts from the very first thing you show participants at the moment of joining your meeting or session.

- Use **visual slides with limited text.** We mention in **Chapter Four** that what goes on in the session, synchronously, should be discussion-based and interactive as far as possible. In other words, do not give your participants too much individual reading that they could do perfectly well in their own time, asynchronously. Not only does it drain energy and motivation to be faced with endless slides conveying information by text, it is not an effective way for people to learn when together in a 'live' session.

  Much has been written and said elsewhere about 'death by PowerPoint'. We won't repeat that here, but just remind you that slides are a different resource when working virtually from in the face to face setting. They are not only important, they are pretty much essential, the backbone of your session.

Slides share ideas, stimulate debate, let people know what they are going to be doing next, and who with. But the most effective slides, we find, in virtual 'live' sessions do so through images, with as few words as possible.

IMAGINATIVE SLIDE DECKS

Here are some great uses for slides to engage your participants visually.

- **Welcome slides** which show a friendly image and create a sense of comfort and ease
- **Reflective slides** which might share, for example, an image from nature which is both attractive to look at, relaxing and engages people in quiet reflection for a minute or two when seeking to generate fresh ideas
- **Symbolic slides** which share information through images alone. One example we sometimes use is an 'Energiser slide' – sharing different ideas for energising participants in virtual sessions. These are conveyed entirely through images rather than words, and participants have to make the connection between the 'symbol'/ image and the idea behind it.
- **Playful 'teambuilding' slides** which invite people to undertake an activity under pressure of time, possibly in competition with another team. One example we sometimes use is a set of slides inviting people to connect different kinds of virtual facilitation 'skill' with an image of an animal that represents it, by connecting the two on slide via some of the annotation tools available on the software platform. This generally elicits plenty of laughter and helps people consider the information in a much less boring way than if we had simply used a slide with a lot of bullet points sharing 'virtual facilitation skills'.
- **Creative 'brainstorming' slides** which invite people to 'tell a story' according to some images supplied, one by one, in front of them. The story may be about anything, but it involves listening to what has been said already, and building on it. It's not difficult to see how this kind of activity can be very helpful in getting fresh thinking behind a new product or service in a project team, or sharing new ideas for a company process, for example.

By now, you may be thinking that such slides do not sound very 'corporate' or business-like. You may be right, and of course it's essential to adjust the content and presentation of your slides to fit with your clients' needs, and company culture.

But we urge you not to let caution entirely rule the day. People are people, wherever you find them, and everyone likes to be shown something slightly different, to have their imagination fired, to engage with ideas and be stimulated in enjoyable ways with the theme of your session. If we always stick with the tried-and-tested, 'safe' and instructive slide in cyber space, we are ignoring the exhilarating possibilities of innovation that this way of working offers.

- **Use photos – yourself, your producer, your participants – on slides** as much as possible in virtual sessions to remind people of your individual and group presence. We mentioned earlier that creating a 'virtual classroom' in the participants' imagination is an excellent way to engage with people and create a certain mood or atmosphere. Of course, how you represent yourself as facilitator via visual images is also important, and sadly leaves a little less space to play. While we may be tempted to put up a photo of Cameron Diaz, Naomi Campbell, Jonny Depp, Eddie Murphy or Shashi Kapoor to represent ourselves, accuracy is best in this case.

Make sure you include a photo of everyone attending the session, including the delivery team, and use the photos on your introduction, check in and any team activity slides. It really does help people remember that we are living, breathing human beings located somewhere in the world, not 'just' disembodied voices talking through technology. It also helps you, as facilitator, remember who is with you and keep everyone involved and included.

A final word here, and this may sound a little silly, but bear with us. If you are working with a group over time and using photo slides – remember to **not always show the photos in exactly the same arrangement each time.** In other words, mix it up a bit. If you are showing two rows of photos (depending, of course, on group size and slide space), make sure the people who have been regularly on the bottom row get 'promoted' sometimes to the top, and vice versa. And **be consistent** – make sure all photos are the same size, of the best possible quality, show people at their best, and where possible show smiling rather than stern faces. You may be going to look at them for weeks on end, so ensuring people feel comfortable with how they are represented is key.

Photos on your slides are the equivalent of seating positions, perhaps even chair size, in the face to face classroom. Suffice it to say that if you want to achieve a sense of equality and fairness among your virtual participants, use photos well and with sensitivity so that all feel fairly represented and included.

Technology

Of all the six aspects of virtual facilitation 'approach', technological mastery is the one we are going to say least about. Partly because we have already said so much in this book. So we include it here as a reminder that knowing how to operate your technology matters, but practice will get you there, and, as you know by now, the services of a technical producer will be of considerable help.

Finally, take heart. Technological failure rarely wrecks your session, as long as you have the skill to and savvy to remain calm, reassuring and flexible with your Plan B.

In this chapter we've had a fairly comprehensive look at the responsibilities, skills and elements that contribute to a virtual facilitator's style and approach. Everything we say here applies equally well to all virtual events, whether training or coaching sessions, or a team meeting.

But meetings are a particular bugbear in corporate life, and virtual meetings have a particularly bad reputation for being seen as ineffective, disengaged, de-energising – bluntly put, a waste of time. In our next, **Chapter Six**, we explore in more depth why this is, what gets in the way of making virtual meetings work, and how to make them go, to borrow from English poet T S Eliot's famous phrase, with a creative 'bang' rather than an ineffective 'whimper'.

References

1) Cune, S., Fogelberg, F., (2011) 'Can Remote Leadership Skills be Learnt?'
2) Campbell, A., Whitehead, J., Finkelstein, S., (2009) Harvard Business Review
   https://hbr.org/2009/02/why-good-leaders-make-bad-decisions
3) Lister, M., Listening (2015). Co-Active Coach Training Newsletter
   http://www.thecoaches.com/coach-training/resources/coaching-tools/listening
4) Caulat, G., (2012). Virtual Leadership. LIbri Publishing
5) Morgan. G., (1993). Imaginisation: New Ways of Seeing and Organising. Sage
6) Eliot, T, S., (1925). The Hollow Men. Faber and Faber

ONLINE MEETINGS

How to avoid being distant while working over distance

6

by Sven Cune, Mara Garofalo, Jude Tavanyar

'Wherever I lay my hat …. I can also run an online meeting' – (with apologies to Billy Joel)

Why virtual meetings are sometimes ineffective

Poorly-run virtual meetings are definitely seen by some as 'even worse' than poorly run face to face ones. In virtual space we have come to know the 'amplification principle', which means that management behaviours, good or bad, get amplified: a good manager looks excellent in virtual space and a bad manager looks awful when working remotely (Gandhi, 2009). The same principle applies to virtual meetings, which is why so many people have such strong feelings about them.

But let's take a step back first.

In **Chapter One** of this book we outlined some of the considerable changes that have taken place in the world of work since the 1980s, not least of them regarding the developing corporate culture of 'flexible working', and, with technological revolution, of the global workplace. These possibilities to communicate 24/7 across the world were once, of course, inconceivable.

The reality is that it is now possible to work almost anywhere, at almost any time, if your energy, phone and Internet connection will allow. Indeed, as we have pointed out, flexible/remote working is not just a bonus, but becoming an absolute requirement of today's business executive or consultant. So flexibility means freedom and autonomy – being able to work when you choose in many cases, and, to a certain extent, how you choose.

Are virtual meetings 'too easy' to arrange and therefore not taken seriously?

But the 'new flexibility' has a price. Evidence suggests that executives find it harder than ever to set boundaries around their work time and effort, given that they are (potentially, at least) available around the clock.

While some 15 to 20 years ago, the 'fixed office base' with its prescribed working hours meant that there was a clear-cut distinction between being 'at work' and 'at home', the possibility to make contact and communicate around the clock may well mean that meetings in general have become 'too easy' to arrange and therefore take place with less consideration of executives' time and less careful planning than previously.

Indeed, combined with the real pressures of performing in a global marketplace where competitor organisations are regularly demanding round-the-clock accessibility from their higher-paid executives, the current culture of the 24/7 workplace may provide an excellent reason why the attractive-sounding notion of 'flexibility' does not, ironically, always result in reduced stress, or a greater sense of autonomy and choice for today's executive.

Working flexibly can be stressful

Our experience as executive coaches suggests that managing work-life balance for many has never been more challenging, a juggling act where the ball that most often gets dropped is that of personal time, away from the computer or phone, and from the endless demands of colleagues and clients.

All of which places certain demands upon anyone who is responsible for communicating with colleagues over distance and time-zones. Communicating and leading remotely involve crucial skills, and the protection of important boundaries around work and personal time so that flexibility does not itself simply add to the burden of executive stress.

Without this consideration of personal time (and time-zone differences) virtual meetings may become a source of resentment to some attendees if they are not focused and tightly-run. At the same time, ONLY focusing on the task at hand in virtual meetings may make them not only less enjoyable, but in the longer-term less effective, because there is no time for people to get to know each other and build professional relationships.

The role of a remote leader is a topic which could fill an entire book on its own. However, much of what a remote leader does is communicate over distance, via meetings. So the question is: how can s/he make meetings of all kinds (long or short, spontaneous or scheduled) effective, stimulating and memorable for all participants? Can virtual meetings even be – yes! – enjoyable and make the best possible use of participants' time? We strongly believe that they can, and at their best, remotely-led meetings can be energising and even inspirational.

In this chapter we will look at:

- Why the 'psychology' – the ideas, theories, individual preferences and choices – behind virtual facilitation matters at least as much as getting the technology right

- Preparing for virtual meetings – a critical list that will help you get the best from your meetings and keep people involved and engaged

- Virtual 'etiquette' – the 'best practice' guidelines and approach during the session to make virtual communication effective and enjoyable

- How to choose meeting 'technology' that fits your needs.

Psychology and technology
There are of course many reasons why **any** badly run meeting – virtual or otherwise – can feel like an irritating waste of time. These include:

- late participants

- an unrealistically full agenda

- no agenda, so people don't know why they're there

- one person dominating the conversation while others barely get a chance to speak

- unclear or non-existent actions and outputs.

In our experience, the reasons why virtual meetings are seen as particularly challenging has to do both with fear of technology, and inadequate application of psychology – in equal measure.

The kind of technological difficulties which a virtual facilitator might expect to come across fairly regularly, but which are far from insurmountable, are dealt with in **Chapter Two**, alongside the more challenging but generally rare moments when no 'Plan B' is possible. We remind you that almost every problem that technology throws up can be dealt with in some way.

And if that sounds hopelessly optimistic, in our experience even the most technically unskilled and fearful facilitators rapidly learn the ropes and become positively innovative in their approach to managing technical challenges. Some even get to enjoy the challenges, finally!

The psychological side – group dynamics in virtual meetings

So while we firmly believe that technology is important, the approach used by the meeting Chair or team leader is also a key factor in achieving success. And that's what we mean when we talk about 'psychology' here– the mood or 'communicative environment' that the meetings Chair is able to create, and the thinking and 'tactics' used to do so.

When people are at geographical distance, and particularly when they are under pressure of time and other priorities this becomes extremely important. Ignore this at your peril – if people feel disengaged and 'turned off' by an unfriendly, overly formal, abrasive or verbose meeting facilitator, then the whole meeting is likely to be unproductive, and in a split second will create a sense of disenchantment about any further meetings of this kind.

Why do we emphasise this? Early on in our experience as virtual facilitators, we noted something a little strange. This was that, for some reason, the basic politeness people show each other when they meet and interact face to face, irrespective of their national culture, is pretty much forgotten when meeting and interacting virtually.

For example – we increasingly notice that in virtual meetings people will often jump straight to the task at hand, without any friendly preliminaries, work through the agenda topics and then log out of the meeting again. In this entire meeting process there are very few conversations taking place that do not relate entirely to work, and, even before the end of the meeting, people may 'leave', without any prior notice or bothering to say goodbye. And perhaps this is not surprising – in far too many virtual meetings, the end of the meeting may be as abrupt as the beginning, with little chat or interaction about anything other than action points and deliverables.

In comparison, what might normally happen in the face to face equivalent of, say, a project team meeting? Usually there is some informal 'chat' and catching up around the coffee machine, as people speak in pairs or small groups about personal interests, opinions on news and external events, even how their love life is developing!

Of course the level of importance of the chat depends on the trust and openness in the group, but this kind of informal, free-flow personal conversation is very important, and people tend to do it instinctively when face to face because it relaxes and helps everyone to 'settle in' and feel welcome in a friendly atmosphere.

What does that have to do with getting work done? A great deal. While this depends to a certain extent upon cultural and personal preferences, not having this 'coffee-style chat' before the 'meeting proper' starts can be detrimental to team spirit. These informal moments turn out to be enormously important in achieving a productive, relaxed atmosphere to create openness and enable 'serious work' to take place.

And, of course, it (almost) goes without saying that leaving a face to face meeting early without a word of warning or goodbye would be taken in a great many situations as rather rude.

Make meetings interactive, relevant and enjoyable

So why do people behave differently with each other when meeting virtually? Probably many reasons, but here are two important ones. Despite the fact we are increasingly used to working virtually, still far too many people sit in virtual meetings, present but somehow not fully engaged. That is partly because that is what we have become used to, with the longstanding webinar tradition of a 'one way presentation' without conversation.

Consequently, participants may feel little commitment to the meeting, and that their presence or absence does not matter too much. It doesn't take much imagination to see that these are the people who generally contribute the least in any meeting, and may remain passively muted, or leave early. The meetings Chair may have to work quite hard to get these participants engaged and contributing actively.

Another reason why people may behave in virtual meetings with little engagement is because online meetings are fairly easy to arrange, as discussed above. As they are far more convenient to set up in many cases than their face to face counterpart, they are sometimes organised on a whim, without proper consideration, and thus over-used. If people are called to meet virtually enough times, and find that the meeting was frankly unimportant, badly run, or not relevant – you can guess the rest. Even if they do show up on future occasions (because they have to), don't expect them to be energised or highly motivated.

And finally, a dull, presentational style from the Chair or team leader, will empty 'virtual seats' very rapidly. On the other hand, a well-planned, interactive approach with a lively exchange of views and perspectives is the best way to get an informative debate with important questions aired and shared.

You may now be reading this list and thinking: 'Well – obviously! But HOW am I supposed to make my virtual meetings so engaging?'

Getting people to take virtual meetings seriously while making them enjoyable, interactive and useful is entirely achievable, both by preparing beforehand, and by applying some basic principles during the meeting itself. So – here's some ideas to get your meetings into top gear and leave people wanting more!

Let's start with the preparation aspect.

Preparing for the meeting

Five Questions to Ask Yourself Before Arranging the Meeting

Before arranging any meeting, it makes sense to ask yourself some key questions. They are:

- Why is this meeting important? Have I made clear why I am calling it?

- Who should I invite? Have I invited the relevant people?

- How should we meet, and have I clarified how we will connect? (See The 'Task-Technology Matrix in **Chapter Two**, for selecting the best technology)

- When should we meet? Have I taken participants' time zones into account and kept the timing as tight as possible?

- What is the purpose of the meeting? Have I created an agenda that will lead to achieving the objective?

- Have I involved appropriate others in building the agenda?

These key questions are reproduced again in a checklist format in the **Resources** section of this book. If the meeting Chair cannot answer all of these practical questions clearly and persuasively, it is time to consider what is getting in the way – before the meeting goes ahead.

Eight Tips for Preparing Successful Virtual Meetings

Being prepared for a virtual meeting is as important as preparing for the face to face variety. While you do not want to be excessively formal in your approach, you do need to be clear and purposeful, and to make good use of everyone's time. (Please note that while there is some overlap with points already mentioned in **Chapter Five**, preparing to run a virtual meeting is not exactly the same as preparing to facilitate or coach virtually. So we have included here the key preparation points for virtual meetings, some which may be familiar by now, and some new.)

PRACTICAL TIPS

- **Work from a quiet place.** We have had meeting participants calling in from taxis, metros, McDonalds and so on – one client we worked with even tried to run an online meeting while his laptop was going through airport security.

A high risk venture indeed, and best avoided, unless you are not only a facilitation expert but also have top-notch diplomacy skills to smooth your colleagues' ruffled feathers!

Getting a private room may not be easy, of course. We often hear stories from clients that they have quite a struggle to get a quiet workspace to log in to an online meeting. But this is very important, not only because it minimises disruptive background noise, but also because participants need to feel free to speak openly and honestly at virtual meetings, without interruption and distraction – just as they would at a face to face meeting.

After all, if you are not in a quiet and private setting as facilitator, attendees may assume that you are not bothering to take the meeting seriously, so why should they?

- **Notify colleagues or family members in advance that you will be in session.** As said above, virtual meetings sometimes tend to be considered as somehow not 'real' meetings. This can result in colleagues disturbing you while in a virtual meeting, assuming that it is OK to do so.

  Put a sign on your door (or, if you really cannot find a private space to work from, somewhere clear beside you on the desk) notifying people that you are running or attending a virtual session. If you also tell people who are likely to interrupt you that you are unavailable and not to be contacted at the time when the meeting takes place, this reinforces the point.

- **Ask all participants to attend from their own (not shared) workstation.** This particular 'ground rule' is often resisted by busy managers. For many executives, it is already hard enough to find a quiet room to work in, and so if you are based in the same workplace as another meeting participant, why not share the work station together?

  Here are some good reasons why we ask people to avoid sharing workstations. Firstly, it is inconvenient. Sharing a standard microphone is not good for the audio 'presence' of either of those sharing, and if they have to resort to using speakerphone in order to avoid sharing the mic, the sound quality will most definitely suffer.

  Secondly, when using some web meeting platform or teleconference services, it is not always possible to tell who is speaking if the microphone is shared – until one gets used to the sound of the speaker's voice. This is confusing and makes everyone's experience a little more challenging.

  Finally – and perhaps most importantly, time and again we hear that when two or more people share a computer or phone line (desktop speaker) to join a meeting, it creates an 'us' and 'them' feeling within the group. In other words, the small group sharing a room together is perceived to be in closer alliance than others in the meeting, as they are not joining the meeting on the same basis as everyone else.

  It really is surprising to what extent the existence of 'sub groups' can have a negative impact on group 'connection' and team performance, if ignored. The challenge is that these subtle group dynamics often occur without being noticed and can cause some disruption and disturbance in the group before anyone has spotted this.

  Telepresence technology, with its sophisticated audio and video features, takes away some of the obstacles to effective remote communication but still does not overcome the point of sub-groups. To avoid this and create a high performing group dynamic, we recommend that every member joins web meetings and phone conferences individually.

- **Use a (USB) headset.** If the meeting platform that you are using allows you to call in using your computer or phone, choose to use a headset. VOIP (Voice Over Internet Protocol) compared to calling in by telephone tends to produce a more clear and 'real' sound when calling into an audio conference.

We recommend a USB headset – one that plugs into the USB portal on your computer – as it produces better sound than a normal 'double jack' headset (a headset with two connectors, one for the microphone, one for the headphones). The connection is more immediate and more reliable.

- **Maximise strength and reliability of your Internet connection:** If you are running a meeting from an Internet platform, aim to be 'plugged in' to your router, not on Wi-Fi. It really makes a difference to signal strength and clarity, particularly if there are numerous other activities run on Wi-Fi taking place around you. And of course, the faster your broadband speed, the greater the quality of the connection.

- **Reduce distractions or clutter in your meeting space.** If you like to have photos, books, papers, stationery, coffee mugs around you when you work now is the time to clear your desk!

- **If you're using webcam, set the scene a little.** While it would be a stretch for most of us, even with fancy lighting and a carefully positioned camera, to turn a cramped home office room into an upmarket-looking conference suite, it is possible to look professional if running your meeting from home, without calling the decorators and de-clutterers in. Check that what is visible (if anything) around and behind you through the lens of the webcam is what you wish meeting attendees to see. A private, well-lit, fairly neutral setting is the best.

Everything in place? Job done? Not quite. The practicalities may all be taken care of, but what about your approach?

If you have never given this much thought before, it's time to consider the general 'principles' and skills involved in making virtual meetings enjoyable and engaging. Whilst being easily understandable and simple to acquire, these may need a bit of practice if you have got used to working in a more formal, structured way with less scope for discussion and spontaneous interaction.

We have referred to the idea of 'virtual etiquette' already in previous chapters. Below, we've listed some principles – meetings 'etiquette', if you like – which may be particularly useful in creating collaborative and successful virtual meetings.

During the meeting

Ten guidelines for successful virtual meetings

Here is a list of guidelines, or 'ground rules', for meetings that we use regularly and that you might like to try too, alongside the preparation points mentioned above. And bear in mind that the list is highly adaptable – why not take some of these ground rules and create your own version from the list for your own team? Some organisations to whom we have proposed this 'virtual etiquette' list have created what they call a 'team charter' or 'team ground-rules', adding to and amending some of the points here.

PRACTICAL TIPS
. . . .

- **Call in 15 – 30 minutes early**. Technology can be unpredictable from time to time. By simply calling in early you will have time to work out any glitches. If you are sharing any documents or slides you need to be sure they are in place so you can show them quickly and easily without wasting time looking for them later in the meeting, that is, if you are using a document-sharing or screen-sharing technology.

   However, there is another reason for being early. In order to set the stage for an open and trusting environment it is also very important that you as Chair log in early and connect with the participants that join early too. It is really surprising to see how much influence just a few minutes of initial informal conversation can have on the rest of the meeting, helping to create a relaxed, open and productive mood which can last throughout the session.

   Participants pick up a great deal when working virtually by the kind of welcome and 'atmosphere' of the first few minutes – it is a subtle cue for them regarding how you as Chair want everyone to experience the meeting, and they usually respond in the same way to you.

- **Set the scene and run through practicalities.** Welcoming all participants in a warm and friendly way is an excellent start, and taking care to introduce any guests or 'new people' on the team to the others, if this is a regular team meeting. Clarify roles – who is the producer (if there is one), the Chair and the 'scribe' for any notes that might be taken and shared via whiteboards, slides, chat box or email etc. Just as in a face to face meeting, clarifying the objectives, agenda and timing is also very important and helps people to feel comfortable and know what is expected.

- **Explain the process for getting technical support.** If you are working with a producer for your meeting, you will of course explain this and introduce him/her at the beginning, letting people know how to contact that person for assistance with any technical problems. However, this is quite a luxury for many busy managers and small-scale meetings and it's far more likely that, in small groups at least, you will be 'running the show' alone. In which case you need to help with any technical problems yourself, or via someone else in the team more technically proficient than you are. Talking about this at the beginning, or before the meeting, helps people feel safe, relaxed and more ready to engage.

- **Tell people HOW you want them to communicate with you.** In other words, how you would like them to respond to or ask questions, interrupt, introduce their ideas, and so on. In some platforms you can use a raised hand tool to ask a question, or interrupt – but for many meetings this is excessively formal, and unnecessary in a small group.

  It really makes a difference if people know they should write their answers in Chat space, or on a whiteboard, or even annotate your slides – or simply speak up without any preamble. If people don't know how (or whether) you want them to respond to your points, you will hear silence – the silence of confusion or boredom.

  A lot of these points relate to individual preference and the style of the meetings leader. However we generally find that a combination of speaking up, and 'public' writing – on whiteboard, slide etc – where all can read it – is a good combination for engaging **all** your meeting attendees. Some people naturally talk less, others more – this combination works for both, as long as they know what's expected of them.

- **Be clear about how to join and leave the meeting.** Explain at the very start of the meeting that you would like people to let you know if they have to leave early, and invite them to say goodbye to everyone rather than just 'disappear' into cyber space. Even if it's just a case of having to go on 'mute', or step away for a moment, you and others can send out a chat message, write on the whiteboard, or even use the icons provided in web platforms when available, to inform the whole group.

Asking a question of someone in a virtual meeting who has actually disappeared offline without telling you is an awkward and slightly annoying experience. The impact on the group is that they generally disengage, and productivity suffers.

- **Be inclusive.** Make sure you provide enough air-time for all. It takes all kinds of people to make an effective virtual meeting – the 'quiet types' who don't speak for the whole session, but come up with their most fantastic idea at the very end, as well as those who rarely stop speaking and tend to drown out everyone else. Ensure you invite responses from people in writing as well as aloud, as stated above – and also take care to include everyone, by name, at certain points in the meeting.

- **Balance structure and spontaneity.** Some team leaders or virtual facilitators may tend to adopt a more 'high control' approach when running meetings over distance, fearing that they will not be able to keep people's attention and meet the planned goals effectively. Ironically, being too controlling in virtual meetings can have the opposite effect to keeping attention – people resist too much direction and may react against it.

So while you do need a certain level of structure to manage any meeting, try also to allow for a certain degree of spontaneous interaction. There are plenty of hints about how to do this in **Chapter Five**, and allowing people some 'open space' to brainstorm and share ideas freely, or setting up virtual breakout rooms to discuss topics at the same time, are two excellent techniques. Whatever your tactics, facilitators the world over know that a bit of flexibility, a friendly facilitation style and some unexpected 'playful' elements take a meeting from tolerable, to positively engaging and fun.

- **Bear in mind language differences.** If you are working internationally, this is a common challenge. Being clear about inviting all participants equally to comment – and ensuring that all points are put clearly, and repeated where necessary, goes a long way to helping people relax and not worry about language differences as much.

One facilitator we know makes a point of **always** inviting participants at the start of any virtual session to let him know straightaway if they have missed something, or if a point has not been clearly conveyed. He does this, even if everyone has the same native language! It's an open, inclusive invitation which then makes it possible for everyone to raise points of clarity, not just leaving the onus on those who are less proficient in the language being spoken. You will find more detail on managing language differences, and other aspects of cultural diversity, in **Chapter Eight**.

- **Balance getting tasks done with building and maintaining relationships.** It's a sad fact. Pressures of time mean that people connecting virtually tend to jump straight to the task without spending much (if any) time on building relationships. Of course every meeting is different, and if you are running an informal group 'catch up' with a team of people who already know each other well, this will be less of a consideration than when, say, you are running a meeting for the first time with a brand new project team, all strangers.

  The tendency, in any virtual meeting, to just 'get down to business' and not bother to see how everyone is or spend any time talking in a sociable and friendly way – is ultimately one that can set up more challenges than it finally solves. People just do not feel the same commitment to the meeting or team unless they have opportunities to get to know their team or group members better, as well as get on with the job in hand. The next item gives you a practical tool to do just that.

- **Do a 'Check-In' and a 'Check-Out'.** Working with project teams running meetings virtually some years back, we noticed what happens when people do not take time to bring a little bit of personal information to the meeting by way of letting everyone know how they are, what they have been up to, and any worries or concerns they may have. The result of NOT having this kind of open, personal exchange – even if just for a minute or two each – is that many teams can start to experience unresolved challenges like demotivation, confusion, sometimes conflict.

  A 'Check-In' and 'Check-Out' process, in our view, is an essential part of virtual etiquette in any meeting. We've described it earlier in **Chapter Four**, and it is a simple 'round-the-table' approach where everyone, in turn, says two or three sentences about how they are feeling, what they are hoping for from the meeting and any particular concerns or support they may need.

CASE STUDY:

AGGRESSIVE MEETINGS IN A REMOTE PROJECT TEAM

Here's one story about what can happen when the meetings Chair does not take time to help the team build relationships and get to know and understand each other. Working with a remote project team – all of whom lived and worked at considerable geographical distance from each other across 4 continents – for an 18 month assignment, it became obvious to the project team Chair that tension and unexpressed grievances were building up in the team.

The team had become very task-focused and little attention had been paid from the start of the project to team-building or helping members make supportive individual relationships with each other. As a result, two members of the team were feeling that they were being ignored by the others, and another, the only woman on the team, spoke of being actively dismissed and interrupted each time she tried to express her view on an agenda item.

In consequence the team were spending a lot of time arguing with each other in a heated but unproductive way, and this was draining time and also causing some project team members to feel exhausted and demotivated. It became so bad for the female member of the team that she contemplated resigning from the process. Finally, she went to the team Chair to share her disappointment and frustration and the Chair addressed the issue with some open discussion about how the team could communicate more effectively and collaboratively over distance.

While these challenges in group dynamics are sometimes part of the team-forming process, if more time had been taken to help the group 'bond' at the beginning of the project, the impact of the negative communication might have been more fleeting and easily managed. As it was also allowed to continue for some time, without any input or attention from the meetings Chair, the destructive, time-wasting effects were exacerbated, until morale for almost all team members dropped considerably.

A key learning point at the end of the project for this team was the high importance of taking time for sociable conversation and inclusive 'rituals' like a Check In process, to create a feeling of closeness, trust and understanding early on. This may seem like another drain on time in the short term. However, as this example shows, it turns out finally to be the very opposite.

A Check-Out, as the name suggests, takes place at the end of the meeting and serves the purpose of giving everyone a moment to say anything that was still left unsaid or undiscussed and bring closure to the meeting. It is swift but friendly and inclusive, with each person speaking interrupted in turn, whether to make a general comment, or in response to a specific question from the meeting Chair.

Of course, if you are working with a big group or team of 25 people or more, there may just not be enough time for everyone to speak in turn in this way. However, virtual platforms offer several different ways to run a Check In and Check Out process via whiteboards, writing on slides, and other techniques, even in larger groups.

- **Ending the meeting and after closure.** Neat closure is as important in virtual meetings as in face to face ones – perhaps even more so. Ensure that agenda points and decisions are summarised and recorded. If you have recorded the meeting – possible with technologies such as WebEx – a link to the full recording may be sent to all participants so they can play back any particular aspects of the meeting as they wish. Make sure that you have a rule for protecting confidentiality in place when recording sessions. If you are recording, consider pausing the recording when controversial, conflictual or personal topics are being discussed.

> '*Spending time on task and relationship will turn a virtual team into a high performing virtual team*'
>
> **(Caulat, 2006)**

Specific topics for the virtual Chairperson

Handling Discussions
Handling discussions smoothly in a virtual meeting naturally includes many of the elements with which you will be familiar from running a meeting when everyone is sitting in the same room. However, following the 'amplification principle' we mentioned at the start of this chapter, it's important to pay special attention to some of the standard elements of good Chairing when working in virtual space,

because the negative effects of poor Chairing (just as the positive effects of skilled Chairing) show up even more powerfully when you are not sitting in the same room as your colleagues and team members.

PRACTICAL TIPS

- Work through the agenda, making sure each point has adequate 'air time'

- Take care to describe each topic or issue so that all attendees are clear on key points

- Invite new information and gather suggestions and solutions from all participants

- Make sure everyone has a say and make sure you invite and include those 'shrinking violets' who tend to remain in the background

- Invite participants to speak, interact and contribute throughout. While this seems obvious, many people settle into a more passive stance than usual in virtual space

- Check repeatedly for clarification and invite questions regularly to ensure everyone is clear and engaged

- While it is important to ensure everyone is included and involved, you will also need to control the discussion at times and make sure it sticks to the topic at hand

- Summarise the main information and action points that come out of the discussion and close the topic, then move on

- Begin and end on time – if this means deferring some points, this should be done with agreement

- And finally, bear in mind that people from different cultural backgrounds have different conceptions of what meetings are for and how they should be run. More on this topic in **Chapter Eight**

Decision-making

Whether you as Chair define the decision making process beforehand or invite the group to 'decide how you will decide', it is helpful to define and clarify this. We give 'virtual decision-making' special attention here because a lot of time can be wasted in any meeting (and feelings can also run high) if the process to achieve decisions is not clear, discussed upfront, and followed fairly. In other words, you have to decide how to decide, and that itself is often no easy decision!

Of course some decisions may be deemed low status, others more important – and this will make a difference to the way you reach a conclusion as a group. Naturally, time and the decision-making preferences of the group are also aspects of this, which is why whole books are dedicated to the topic of corporate decision-making. And here too, the cross cultural angle comes into play.

Many meeting platforms offer a polling feature, which gives a virtual meeting an advantage over a face to face one. Making decisions anonymously may be beneficial sometimes, for instance when the hierarchy may prevent members to vote publicly on a decision. Or when the topic at hand is very sensitive. When you set up a poll in such a way that the answers from the participants remain anonymous, only the aggregated results of the whole group will be shown.

Other, more public decision-making tools offered in some platforms enable a green tick or red cross feature to be selected by each participant, among a range of other feedback tools, to signify a 'yes' or 'no' vote. These generally show the individual voter's name and therefore are not appropriate for decisions which need discretion and privacy. In the **Resources** section we include a decision making process called 'Fist to Five' which works very well in a virtual setting.

The Quick 'Drop-In' Meeting

To conclude this chapter, one very appealing aspect of virtual working that we hope you will explore with your colleague and contacts (if not already doing so) is the quick spontaneous exchanges of information and sociable interaction which can take place – the 'quick drop in' meeting. You don't need to plan and organise a full group or team meeting for these, and there is – of course – no scheduling involved.

The ability to use a platform like Skype or Lync to see when someone is available, send a text to connect via audio (and webcam perhaps) for a 5 minute update or sociable exchange is often energising, motivational and saves endless time where an email might have caused more confusion and delay. Spontaneous exchanges, both social and task-focused, are very important in enabling high performing teamwork among people significantly spread in location who may not have the time or need for a longer meeting, but just want a quick 'check in' chat.

British novelist E M Forster famously wrote: 'Only connect!' (Forster, 1910). If he were alive today he might have added: 'In as many different ways as people need to understand, be inspired and fully involved in what you have to say'. Of course the Internet was not in existence when Forster died, but some 50 years later, this famous quotation seems a pretty good message for virtual facilitators the world over.

Now you've got virtual meetings sorted out, how are you going to deal with some of the more 'challenging' (dare we say 'difficult') attendees who may join them? If you're not sure, **Chapter Seven** is all about dealing with diverse audiences.

References

1) Gandhi, N. www.freshbusinessthinking.com
2) Caulat, G., (2006). Virtual Leadership, Learning to Lead Differently, Libri
3) Forster, E. M., (1910). Howard's End

VIRTUAL COMMUNICATION WITH DIVERSE AUDIENCES | 7

By Fredrik Fogelberg

Introduction

In previous chapters, we have looked at the possibilities that technology offers to facilitate human interaction over distance and we have also discussed how people learn in virtual space, and how to design and facilitate learning sessions and meetings that will have the impact you wish.

Now it is time to look at the variety of participants in virtual facilitation events. In doing that, we want to be honest, but not to offend. If you are a resistant and risk-averse senior manager, a highly talkative participant, or one who likes to remain silent but adds considerable value on the occasions when she does speak – we hope you will not feel irritated to be included in a list of potentially 'challenging' candidates for the virtual facilitator!

Our stereotypes are simply included to make a point that certain ways of communicating in virtual sessions can make life tricky, especially for the novice facilitator. In this chapter we include some practical tips and examples to help you charm even the most disengaged participant.

So here are some ideas you may find useful to shape your approach to participants who may present you with a challenge – and help you connect with them effectively. In most cases, it really is a question not of 'how to cope with tricky customers?', but of 'how to accommodate a range of different needs?'

The participant who is afraid of technology

And this participant, ladies and gentlemen, is really almost ANYONE you might meet in your online sessions – before they get properly used to working virtually. However – although this is rare – unfortunately some participants just don't get beyond their fear of technology, which inhibits them from fully using and enjoying the opportunities of working remotely with counterparts or colleagues. They often see virtual working as something they 'have to do', rather than something which offers a world of opportunities with numerous practical benefits, enabling them – at the same time as they get work done – to build meaningful and satisfying working relationships across distance.

This lack of comfort with the virtual environment often results in people acting in a distant or formal manner, with little engagement with others, or the task at hand. It's as if the fearful participant becomes so apprehensive about mastering the technology and keeping everyone engaged (and, let's face it, technical 'glitches' can be a real headache) that they forget their own skills and natural ability to engage people and become 'frozen' into a stiff and unnatural way of communicating.

How to deal with this?

PRACTICAL TIPS

....

- Calmly explain that technology problems **happen** – to everyone

Of course it is important to know how to prevent technology failure, and how to deal with any technological problems 'on the fly' – and that is a key reason for involving a producer in your sessions; *Chapters Two* and *Three* of this book are therefore an important read. However, we strongly believe that this (sometimes obsessive) focus on technology has become an unhelpful distraction for some facilitators, as well as for the fearful participant. People who are nervous about making technological errors or showing incompetence in front of the group can be disruptive in two ways – they may either disengage (for fear of looking foolish if they 'make a mistake') or simply panic when something goes wrong, so that supporting them through any technical difficulties becomes a longer process than it needs to be.

The reality is that experience and skill can never completely rule out technological challenges. Even the most experienced facilitators can and do lose control of their sessions sometimes due to technology failing to work as intended. And this is a very important message for virtual facilitators to convey to all participants, technophobes or technophiles, and to demonstrate in their own delivery.

Be calm, relaxed and ready to 'go with the flow', improvise, fill in time, and find ways to communicate with people when, for example, your own audio is not working. Talking about this, and demonstrating it, are both powerful ways of relaxing those who have become somewhat 'hung up' on their latent fear of technology.

- **Include a technology 'warm up' session in an ongoing programme of events**

In *Chapter Six*, we discuss the importance of running a 'kick-off' or introductory session for participants who will be meeting or learning together online over a period of time. Designing and delivering a 'warm up' session before the first 'official' contact takes place is an excellent opportunity for people to get used to the technology and way of working without 'freezing up' through fear of looking technologically incompetent in front of others during the team meeting or learning event itself.

- **Include individual technology checks beforehand**

We have also said this before (in *Chapter Two*) but it's worth repeating. Although conducting individual technology checks does take up time, it is worth every second you or your producer spend on it. By contacting participants one to one in advance of the event (especially if it's an ongoing programme, and particularly if they are new to interactive online events) you help them understand what they can do to have the smoothest connection to the session and the best sound quality once they've joined it. You also have the chance to help them relax and feel comfortable with you as facilitator or producer. That will result in a more enjoyable meeting or learning programme for them, and potentially less disruption for you.

Some facilitators do not see the need to do an individual 'tech' check for a single, 'one-off' meeting. That is of course understandable and is unnecessary with people who are familiar with meeting virtually.

But we would suggest that for any group that includes 'novices' as well as those experienced in communicating virtually, and especially if the group is sizeable (eg more than 10 people) – it is worth doing a pre-session / programme technology check every time.

▪ **Take Questions and Answers both in-session and offline**

One of the worst ways of dealing with the 'technophobe' participant is to ignore him or her. If you have a group and one person is constantly asking questions about technology, and not having their questions addressed – the questions and concerns are unlikely to go away, but the person might.

It is always a good idea to make time for Q and As on any related topic in your sessions. Be careful to keep the timing tight so that you do not run out of time, and also invite questions that can be dealt with offline – via email, for example – and shared, with the responses on your group webpage or bulletin board. In our experience Q&A sessions keep energy and interaction high, if well-managed and timed – they also help people to relax and get the most out of the session, if they know they will have a chance to discuss their technological and other queries and concerns.

▪ **Working with time-challenged senior managers**

We have trained numerous groups of senior and middle managers on the topic of how to lead a virtual team, and in doing so, we notice a few recurring trends. One is that ease with technology is not necessarily related to the hierarchical level of participants. In fact, it's sometimes the opposite – we have often experienced very senior managers who turned out to be novices when it comes to using fairly simple equipment such as a headset, an annotation tool or a chat box.

In many ways, this is quite understandable – the more senior a leader gets in an organisation, the more s/he gets used to having assistance and support in IT matters. So they may simply not be used to managing online communication platforms themselves. However, this can present a challenge to virtual facilitators at times, especially when this lack of experience is coupled with the additional challenge that, the more elevated in rank the executive, the less time s/he has to acquire new skills and competencies – in the virtual environment or elsewhere.

When we throw into the mix the realities of role-related pressure, deadlines and responsibilities, the stress-driven and time-starved manager can become a somewhat 'high maintenance' prospect for the virtual facilitator, expecting maximum value in minimum time. Unfortunately for both, the manager may not necessarily have the technical competence or composure to make it easier for the facilitator to deliver that combination smoothly and effectively.

Of course this may sound like a stereotypical portrait of senior leaders who find themselves needing to acquire virtual communication skills in a very short time. And, forgive us – to a certain extent it is. However it is a reality that at some point in your career as a virtual facilitator, it really helps to know some of the challenges these leaders face because almost inevitably some of those challenges will impact upon you, the facilitator, if you don't take them into account.

- **Creating a safe space for others to experiment and learn from mistakes**

As *Chapter Four* clarifies, there is plenty of evidence behind the idea that adult learning generally thrives best in a calm environment where there is room to experiment and make mistakes. Creating a playful and relatively risk-free environment for senior managers and others who may not feel comfortable to acknowledge their lack of expertise is a first step for you as their facilitator.

And this may be challenging, yes, but in our experience is really no 'mission impossible' for the talented facilitator. The key here is to stay patient, not let oneself be provoked by others' impatience and openly-voiced disgruntlement at times, and to approach the participants with an inclusive and non-judgemental attitude. The resistance will usually then gradually fade.

Not all participants bring this attitude of fear and high expectations in combination, so the skilled facilitator can use the positive energy of the more upbeat and motivated participants to slowly build a healthy learning climate.

- **Aim to create an atmosphere of trust and openness**

The debate about whether it is possible to really establish trust with a group of strangers over a telephone or Internet connection has been running for some time. Our view – no surprises here – is that it most definitely is, with a sensitive and respectful approach which welcomes open discussion of needs and feelings whilst providing a safe clear structure for each session, with in-built flexibility.

Every facilitator and producer has their own unique approach to running virtual events. Whatever that is, you are likely to need to communicate to others how you intend to work with them – something we refer to as 'virtual etiquette', or the 'rules of play' for effective learning and communication in cyber space.

Chapter Six on virtual meetings says more about aspects of virtual etiquette. What we suggest here is that you are explicit from the beginning of a programme or meeting regarding what your participants can expect from you – your 'approach' or 'modus operandi' – and what you would like from them, regarding how they communicate during sessions. This really is of great importance in helping people relax and developing a trusting atmosphere where differences can be addressed and challenges or complaints raised in an open and respectful way.

- **Show respect and integrity and involve regular two-way feedback**

Role-modelling your own 'virtual etiquette' or rules by showing the principles in your own communication with participants is a very powerful way to reinforce the kind of atmosphere and learning environment you seek to establish.

A further strategy to achieve that kind of trusting communication is by introducing the idea of feedback exchanges early on, so that participants know there will be specific opportunities to give practical, respectful comments – appreciative or constructive critique – at particular times throughout the meetings or learning programme.

Establishing a culture of practical and respectful feedback takes some work and effort as for some participants it may not feel natural or comfortable to be direct and clear in this way. In some corporate, and national, cultures feedback is a rather unusual, even risky, communication process.

However there is always some scope for exploring different ways of giving feedback in any group, and it can offer an excellent way to help people cope with new challenges and accept new approaches. Once giving and receiving feedback becomes the norm in any group who meet online at regular intervals, people can review and fine-tune the way they communicate constantly in an open and supportive atmosphere.

The are many ways of giving and receiving feedback when communicating online. In our *Resources* section at the back of this book we include some useful models and tactics.

- **Make virtual facilitation enjoyable; more than 'second best'**

In *Chapter Five* about developing your own style as a virtual facilitator, we talk more about what 'more than second best' means when working with people who may see online meetings as a nuisance and poor substitute for the 'real thing' of face to face presence. We believe there are plenty of people who view it in this way, and managers who have become used to travel and accommodation budgets for international conferences and meetings may not feel 100% thrilled when they are invited to experience its budget-reduced relative, the online meeting.

Of course, many senior executives are delighted by the reduction in travel that online meetings make possible – they see it as a blessing that improves their work-life balance.

However, for some managers and leaders there is a reluctance to 'let go' of some of the privileges that virtual communication renders unnecessary, not least the freedom to plan their own trips away, or the budget to support such trips.

If you become aware that any of your participants are resisting the virtual process because they dislike having to let go of the old ways of working within their company, you are facing a tough challenge indeed, but not an insurmountable one. We have found that, overtime, creating an upbeat and enjoyable mood in your meetings or training events makes a huge difference in winning around the intransigent manager whose mind is focused on the perks of the past, rather than the many benefits that virtual meetings can bring.

The silent participant

In each group, whether meeting face to face or in virtual space, there are some participants that are 'verbal' and like to talk and some that simply do not. This can depend on several factors: personality, culture, group dynamics and motivation.

There is no golden rule in virtual meetings that everyone should participate equally. Trying to achieve that as a facilitator may result in a stilted, unnatural dynamic where people may feel embarrassed. It is more effective to think about what creates an effective balance between the talkers and the more silent participants, and to use the dynamic in a natural and productive manner.

PRACTICAL TIPS

- **Be aware of and cater for personality differences**

Using the 'Big 5' model (Goldberg, 1990) to look at personality, we can, for instance, distinguish between more introverted and more extraverted characters. In a group, introverts tend to process information by thinking things through ('going inside') and extraverts have a preference for talking things through ('going outside'). Both are equally valuable, but different, and involve different kinds of contributions to a learning group.

It is therefore helpful to understand when facilitating virtually that an introvert's silence may not mean she is bored or disengaged. It may mean that the participant is thinking in depth about an idea that she may feel willing to share only when it is polished and developed. In contrast, a clear extravert by preference may not worry about fine-tuning thoughts and suggestions before offering them, and hence moments of silence are likely to be somewhat short-lived with this personality type.

- **Design for diverse preferences**

The conclusion from this is that a virtual session design needs to take in account both introverted, extroverted (and other) preferences – by providing time to reflect and write on the one hand, and opportunity to discuss and talk on the other.

We also see that introverts tend to enjoy speaking up more in small groups whereas clear extraverts are often happy to speak up in a group of any size. For this reason, so-called 'break out spaces' in virtual meetings are often highly appreciated by all participants, extroverts and introverts alike, and the output of the meeting will increase by offering this opportunity.

- **Be ready for and work with cultural communication differences**

In some cultures active and verbal participation in virtual meetings is seen as desirable and positive, whereas in other cultures it is polite to be silent until asked by the leader or superior to speak. In the latter kind of culture, speaking up involves the risk of insulting or embarrassing someone, so silence often feels like the safer option for such participants.

Speaking is silver, silence is golden. Mahatma Gandhi started the spiritual practice of being silent one day a week. He chose Mondays; a habit that he continued while he was head of state for India and until his death.

The virtual session leader needs to think about how to involve participants from all cultures without causing embarrassment. The starting point should be what is appropriate and comfortable for each culture represented. For instance, participants from a highly hierarchical culture will contribute more through a poll or in small groups, than in an open group discussion where there are more hierarchical 'levels' of people participating.

The topic of cultural differences in virtual groups is discussed in **Chapter Eight**.

- **Try to find out whether your participants are motivated**

And finally, the thorny issue of 'motivation' may offer some answers to why one or two of your participants are disengaged in your online event.

If you're struggling to know how to overcome the 'silence' you typically hear from these participants, ask yourself some questions:

- What is participation actually for, in this group?

- Have participants chosen to attend, or are they obliged to?

- Might they regard the meeting as a means of 'helping' them with a particular area of skills development where they currently under-perform, or might they regard attendance as a privilege?

- Are they happy to make time for this meeting or is their silence signalling that they would rather spend their time elsewhere?

These are tough questions and worth considering because the assumptions participants make about what any virtual meeting can or cannot bring them is likely to shape their reactions at the beginning of such meetings.

The level of motivation participants bring to any session depends – let's face it – on you. It particularly depends on your ability to show people that your meeting or training or team session brings valuable, interesting insights into any particular topic. It also depends on your ability to help people to get to know each other, interact, and learn, not just from you but from each other also.

- **Check your own attitude to silence**

If you as a virtual facilitator are afraid of silence, and worry when you hear nothing but your own voice trying to fill that silence – then you are not well-placed to deal with the challenges it throws up. There are plenty of occasions when working virtually that silence – as suggested above – is an indicator of reflection and deep (cerebral) engagement, as well as a cultural gesture of politeness and respect to you, perhaps.

And … you guessed … there are plenty of times when the silence simply means people are bored, and looking at their emails – or even making slightly rude comments about you in the Chatbox. What to do?

- **Silence happens. Get used to it**

Get comfortable with silence, because you will hear it. Working with any group over time, you will get to understand and feel relaxed with the unspoken communication of the group – the non-verbal sounds, intonations and silences that tell you what may be happening.

Find out what kind of silence it is

If at any time you hear a silence, and you are genuinely concerned about what it shows, be confident enough to question it, with a simple query or comment. For example – 'I'm hearing silence – is everyone OK?' or 'Can I assist or clarify something?' Or: 'A response would be appreciated, a simple "yes" or "I have understood" – thank you'.

Whatever happens, do NOT shout: 'Is anyone actually listening to me out there?' (It won't help.)

Simple questions inviting feedback are often a very useful device for understanding the mood behind what you hear, especially when working in the absence of any visual clues.

These considerations both help you develop sessions where silence may not only be unavoidable, but may also even play an important and positive role, particularly when time to think and generate new ideas is needed.

The talkative participant

So now you know how to facilitate your way through 'cyber silence', what do you do about its opposite – the talkative participant who thinks that taking more than their fair share of air time means being productive in a meeting? And of course, in some contexts, a talkative person can be a real bonus, because s/he provides energy, and the enthusiasm can be infectious to other group members.

However, just as the silent participant can be a challenge for the virtual facilitator, so can the person who never stops talking. Not only that, s/he can also be severely irritating to other participants.

The skilled virtual facilitator knows how to balance the enthusiasm and expressiveness of the talkative participant with the needs of the other members of the group. And this really is a kind of balancing act, in order to keep the whole group engaged and 'switched on'.

There are different ways to manage that balance technologically. Here are some of them.

PRACTICAL TIPS

- **Vary the meeting / learning activities regularly and rapidly**

Blessed with a toolbox of features in the virtual classroom, the virtual facilitator has really got more tricks at her disposal than the face to face facilitator.

As we have seen in **Chapter Four**, a clever design for virtual sessions is characterised by a mix of different features. So, after 10 or 15 minutes of group discussion, it is time for an activity on the whiteboard, poll, with a video clip or in break out rooms. If you are moving fairly swiftly between activities in this way, the design of your session will naturally limit the amount of air time that the talkative participant can claim, to everyone's benefit.

- **Use the mute button – judiciously – whilst still allowing interaction**

Other options to control the flow of the session (and not allow one person to dominate) relate to the 'mute' button. If that sounds rude, read on – we do not mean simply pressing the mute button on that talkative participant … even when you feel tempted. (While this can indeed be done technically, it is rather inadvisable if you are hoping to get good evaluations from your students!)

However, we do suggest putting people on mute 'by default' in larger groups of more than 12 people – but not, of course, keeping them all on mute throughout the session!

While we recommend as a matter of very high importance that you, the facilitator, welcome and enable interaction and spontaneity as far as possible, the likelihood is that the more people who are involved in any session, the more chance there is also that distracting background noise will creep in and disturb the whole group.

If working in a big group with muted participants, people will need to ask for permission to speak, for instance by using a raised hand icon, writing in the chat space, or through a Q&A feature. The facilitator or producer can in this way monitor requests for speaking and act as a kind of 'traffic police' controlling how much 'air time' any particular participant receives. That means that you, the facilitator, will have more control of the session with this kind of an arrangement, and therefore be able to manage the 'over-talkative' types.

Of course the point about balance must be repeated – keeping participants on mute, even in a big group, is not a recipe for high engagement. Make sure they have plenty of opportunities for interaction via the tools mentioned above, and also opportunities to speak at intervals through the session. But you may wish to structure that so that you invite comments from the quieter ones, rather than leave the 'space' open for the talkative types to dominate.

- **Explain the rules at the beginning and be assertive**

If the facilitator has taken the trouble to establish the 'rules of play', or virtual etiquette, these will enable a sense of interaction, engagement and inclusion. And if the expressive participant who is 'managed' by technological controls such as the mute button does not enjoy this, it may finally be just too bad. To be brutally honest, there are circumstances in which, despite patient explanations, some highly expressive attendees may not wish to be quiet.

In those circumstances it is better to quietly and discreetly cope with their annoyance via muting them (with a gentle explanation via chat space if necessary) than to allow them the chance of derailing the session when the rest of the group become bored and 'switch off'.

Which highlights another key difference between facilitation in a face to face and in a virtual setting. And that is that the facilitator has rather less time to take action before participants disengage from what is happening and decide to tune out. In a meeting room participants will at least pretend they are interested and stay in the room, but of course there is no such need in virtual space, where the step to another Window on their computer is just a mouse click away. (To say nothing of the possibility of leaving the computer and making a coffee without being seen!)

- **Let technology take the strain sometimes …**

We have already mentioned the impact of cultural differences in deciding how to cope with a silent participant, and the same goes for a very talkative one. These distinctions apply also regarding, say, the seniority of group members- whether it is deemed appropriate to interrupt a senior leader or follow a strict protocol regarding who gets the 'last word' – these are all aspects of cultural difference which it pays to be aware of, and adjust to in your facilitation.

For the facilitator working regularly with international groups, a significant degree of cultural awareness, understanding and attunement is appropriate. See ***Chapter Eight***.

A shorter-term approach, if you find yourself in a delicate position and do not wish to cause offence by interrupting a senior (but extremely long-winded) participant – is to fall back on technology. Yes, our old friend the alarm clock. Setting the alarm clock on your own, or the producer's mobile device means that it will ring when a person's time is 'over' and it's time for the next person to speak. This is a simple and elegant way for the facilitator to interrupt the speaker without having to do it himself. No more worries about upsetting people. Let technology take the strain.

The resistant participant

You may notice participants in your session who wish they were doing something else – just as in the face to face training session or meeting – unless you are an extraordinarily gifted and experienced trainer who can keep everyone engaged 100% of the time. So – how do we know when people are fantasising about sitting on a deckchair on a beach somewhere, or – a more depressing comparison perhaps, about opening all those emails cluttering their Inbox?

We usually know that this person 'is not really there' because s/he is not responding to questions or is complaining or showing resistance. As communications theorist and writer Paul Watzlawick tells us 'It is impossible not to communicate' (Watzlawick, 1967) – and in virtual space every little sigh of boredom or irritation can be communicated even more noticeably than when working face-to-face.

Here are some practical ideas for dealing with someone who would probably rather be somewhere else. In some cases, perhaps ANYWHERE else.

PRACTICAL TIPS

- **Use a friendly approach and help the person feel valued**

The participant may have a very valid reason for not wanting to be in your session. She may be working under a tight deadline, be uninterested in the topic or have had a 'bad experience' recently with a web meeting. S/he may even – and yes, this has sometimes happened! – have attended the wrong meeting by mistake and wonder how to leave and go to the correct web link.

What to do? There are a number of possibilities here. Try, even if you feel frustrated, to show respect to the person by avoiding arguments or putting pressure on him or her. Early in the session, making the person feel welcome and a valued participant may just help to get them more relaxed and responsive to the session activities.

- **Check what may be causing the resistance**

Try to work out what is causing the resistance. Are your slides due for a make-over, a bit on the text-heavy side? Are you speaking in a particularly boring voice today, or simply far too much? Are you inviting interaction and varying the activities frequently? Are you seeking feedback regularly? Asking for questions and comments along the way helps people to understand that this is an open and friendly place to challenge and be honest in a trusting way.

- ▪ **Run a Check In and get expectations out in the open**

From a design perspective, the Check In round that we always run when the session starts (see ***Chapter Four***) will give the participant a voice very early on and the sense of having a place in the group. The opportunity to express her state of mind and her expectations may surprise her at first, but should quickly help her to settle in.

Hearing the participant's expectations will, in turn, give the facilitator the opportunity to respond in a factual way and say which will of these be met and which are outside the scope of the session. This is a simple method, but it can have a significant effect.

- ▪ **Negotiate some other options**

If the participant overtly expresses her lack of interest, time or energy during the Check in, the facilitator can negotiate options that do suit her agenda, such as attending another session or accessing the session later, as a recording to listen to in her own time. If, however, the participant continues to express openly her reluctance to participate, the facilitator's best option is to simply make sure to include her in all activities, and avoid getting pulled into any 'psychological games'.

- ▪ **Have a private 1:1 conversation**

This is a good idea if you are likely to be working with the participant over time. It is also a good idea even if you are not, because you do not wish any of your clients to leave unhappy, even if virtual working really does not fill them with interest or enthusiasm in the way it does you.

Some things cannot be discussed in the 'big group' setting – so if you sense that the participant may like to have some time to discuss her resistance with you, and that you may be able to help her get used to the session – arranging a time for a quite chat online or by phone is an excellent idea. It also shows you are professional, and seeking the best outcome for everyone.

- ▪ **Finally, 'keep calm and carry on'**

Treating everyone with consideration and thoughtfulness is of course always important. Refusing to get 'thrown' by the one or two people who do not want to 'tune in' to what's on offer is the calm and sensible response of a polished virtual facilitator, whatever your level of experience.

So – following the old adage that it is 'impossible to please all of the people all of the time' – the best a facilitator can do with an insistently disengaged participant is to stay calm and confident, try the measures mentioned above and keep including the person. If none of this seems to make a difference, try not to dwell on the matter further. You have done all you can, and it is time, to MOVE ON.

Be careful of 'over-interpretation'

This tip applies for any kind of participant, not just resistant ones. It is possible for any facilitator working virtually to sometimes 'get it wrong' and over-interpret the audio clues we get when working without webcam. Sighs, yawns, coughs, interruptions – all of these can be disconcerting if they lack visual information, and it is fairly easy to 'over-interpret' a sharp intake of breath or bored-sounding voice and assume that we are boring people, or that they would like to be doing something else.

THE 'GROUP FROM HELL' – A CASE STUDY

Virtual facilitation can be intensely satisfying, but sometimes things just don't work out.

Here's one example from our experience. We trained a group of managers from Europe and Asia on how to lead geographically dispersed teams. The company wanted to save on the travel budget and also increase efficiency by communicating more quickly than before, with their senior executives spending a great deal of their time travelling by air to get to meetings, training events and so on. Another factor that persuaded the company to invest in training on leading remote teams was the fact that their key market competitors are relatively expert in working virtually, and so the company considered it a competitive advantage to gain the same skills.

People in this company are used to doing business face to face over coffee and lunches, and also enjoying the privileges associated with business travel. So, motivation for using the technology and experimenting with new approaches to teamwork was limited from the start.

As a result, we had to put up with participants arriving late in our virtual classroom and also experiencing what seemed like endless problems with the technology. Although a clever bunch, it took some of them 6 sessions to figure out how to use a headset.

On top of this, the regular travel done by most people in this group meant that some tried to join our online meetings while in taxis, underground trains, standing in the security line at airports, from hotel rooms with unreliable WiFi, and, on limited occasions, while actually driving their car!

In virtual space, 'meta' language or non-verbal communication becomes all too charged with meaning, if we are less than confident or have a tendency to self-criticise. Of course it does have meaning, but let's not get carried away and become over-analytical. If we establish the kind of training or meeting environment where openness and respect are welcome, with any luck people will feel able to offer their honest comments and share their reactions openly, especially if you ask them to.

Is the time right for remote working in this group's business?
So, what were the learning points for us? In the case we describe here, we believe that part of the difficulty our facilitators faced was that the timing of the training was simply inappropriate for this group of people and their business. The culture was not quite ready for a full-on entry into working virtually.

Why do we think this? In our experience, people get used to certain things which become embedded in the culture of the company, and so changing the 'mindset' and 'approach' may take longer than you think.

Virtual working is about culture change

We concluded from this experience that helping people to make the transition to virtual working is more than just about providing skills training. In some cases, such as the one above, it really is akin to introducing a culture change. This requires an 'organisational change' approach rather than just a simple training programme.

Following this, we might now include the some additional elements when working with a company whose 'culture' is not fully geared up for virtual communication. These might include some or all of:

PRACTICAL TIPS

- Inviting key executives as 'role models' for the desired behaviour change (managing remotely)

- Establishing a solid IT infrastructure to enable virtual communication

- Rewarding remote leaders in the appraisal and bonus system

- Creating a group of early adaptors as 'change agents', to create movement and enthusiasm in the organisation

- Creating a design team to co-build the training programme. We might, for instance, invite into the team some of the critical voices in the organisation. Changing individual's habits and behaviours requires us to prepare for resistance, and take into account what interventions may be appropriate for the change in culture and behaviours that you are introducing. The intervention needs to become embedded in the culture of the organisation itself, so that it becomes part of, as the phrase goes, 'how we do business around here', a natural and comfortable process that everyone understands and subscribes to. If this does not happen, the changes proposed will remain peripheral and in the longer term, may become unsustainable.

From 'challenging' individuals to cross-cultural challenges

In this chapter we have looked at working with various types of challenge from participants in sessions. In our next, **Chapter Eight**, we go deeper into the skills that are required by communicators who seek to work globally in the virtual world – focusing particularly on cross-cultural theories and skills across continents. For any virtual facilitator who works with international or multi-cultural groups, being aware of how cultural differences can play out in virtual settings is a 'must'.

REFERENCES

1) Caulat, G. (2012). Virtual Leadership. Libri Publishing

2) Goldberg, L (1990). Personality Factor Structure. Journal of Personality and Social Psychology Volume 59, # 6, 1216

3) Watzlawick, P. (1967). Pragmatics of Human Communication. Addison Wesley

CROSS-CULTURAL ASPECTS OF VIRTUAL FACILITATION

8

By Fredrik Fogelberg

Introduction

In this chapter, we look at some questions that have rarely been addressed in any depth within the context of virtual communication. These include:

- How to manage the virtual meeting or event where participants from different parts of the world join the meeting, possibly speaking a language that is their second or even their third, rather than their mother tongue?

- What are the cross-cultural differences and distinctions that may typically 'play out' during a virtual meeting, and how do we handle cross-cultural diversity as a facilitator or chairperson?

- Why is intercultural difference an important topic, and to what extent does it play an influential role in virtual meetings and training sessions?

This chapter seeks to answer these questions in some depth and to provide some good-sense, practical tips that will be universally applicable, whatever the cultural context. We also look at the competencies required by a successful virtual facilitator working across cultures, and suggest actions and behaviours that will enhance your skills and make a positive impact in general.

Let's start with the last question from those above. Does culture matter when working virtually? The simple answer is 'Yes, but'. The 'but' lies in the view that how cultural differences manifest themselves in the dynamics of a virtual group, differs from how they manifest in a collocated group dynamic. Caulat (2012) describes it like this, based on her own research:

'The cultural dimensions, for example the ones defined by Hofstede (1991) or Trompenaars and Hampden-Turner (1997), are not necessarily proving to be relevant in virtual space. Different dimensions seem to become more relevant: the use of silence or the different ways in which 'trust' can be generated. I have learnt that it actually can be counter-productive to focus too much on the multi-cultural character of a group. Stereotyping people based on their national culture might be even more detrimental than in the face-to-face situation.'

As authors we believe that the cultural rules that we have been brought up with through all the groups we belong to, from childhood onwards, are, it is argued, just too powerful to be entirely left behind when we meet in virtual space.

These 'cultural groups' include family, community, village or town, language, schools, clubs, sports, political groups, work places and all the other collectives in which you have ever been a part. And each of these has their own implicit and explicit 'rules' of communication and relationship-building, hierarchy of influence and status, and deep-rooted values and guiding principles. It is hard to see how the subtle and often deeply-hidden impact and influences of these values and principles fails to operate simply because those communicating are not sitting in the same room, and may not be able to see each other.

Taking a common example from my own practice as a virtual facilitator, I have noticed that some people who may be reluctant to speak up in a face to face meeting, may speak more freely in a phone conference or web meeting. One possible explanation of this is that when the boss is not physically present, the hierarchy in a group or team may be less apparent and thus exert less influence on the conversation that takes place.

If this observation is correct, it might be particularly noticeable in the behaviour of participants from a so-called 'high power distance' culture where a specific hierarchy of status and hierarchical position governs what can be said, and how, in conversations with superiors and others (Hofstede, 1991). Similarly, people may speak more directly when – as is the case in virtual meetings, of course – there are fewer ways to express oneself through body language or other visual clues. Such visual 'hints' may be subtle indeed in face to face meetings, but nevertheless say a great deal – ranging from the positioning of colleagues in the room, to who gets to pour and serve the coffee during the meeting. These subtleties that are so obvious in face to face meetings are particularly important in so called 'high context cultures', where the **context** – how things are said and done, by whom, and when – is at least as important as the words themselves (Hall, 1983).

Of course, there are many different elements that give a message meaning in both high and low context cultures. But we find it difficult to accept that, just because visual cues may be missing in virtual space, that the subtle and unspoken 'code of behaviour' that creates an important context for the message in 'high context' cultures becomes entirely unimportant when working virtually.

In the next section of this chapter, we will take a brief tour of what 'cultural diversity' means, and review which elements play out most prominently in the virtual meetings and events in which you participate. If you are already familiar with these cultural dimensions, you may consider skipping the introductory paragraph to each of the four dimensions and go to the last paragraph for each of them, describing the consequences for the virtual facilitator.

Key Aspects of Cross-Cultural Diversity in Virtual Communication

A large number of so-called cross cultural dimensions have become popular through authors like Edward Hall (1983), Geert Hofstede (1991) and Fons Trompenaars (1997). These have proven useful for a wide audience to understand cultural differences from a work perspective, leading to more productive teamwork, improved negotiations, less conflict and better leadership practices.

From our experience in facilitating virtual meetings and training sessions, we have found the following 4 dimensions particularly helpful in understanding the needs and values of intercultural audiences.

- Dimension One – Communication: direct or indirect?
- Dimension Two – Hierarchical or Egalitarian?
- Dimension Three – Task or Relationship: which comes first?
- Dimension Four – Time: Linear or Cyclical?

Dimension One – Communication: direct or indirect?
The way people communicate varies markedly across (business) cultures. In so called 'low context cultures' (Hall,1983), the message tends to be in the words themselves.

What you 'hear' is what you get. Words are used to produce a straightforward and clear message, with no 'packaging'. In low context cultures, to be direct and transparent with others is therefore a value, as in, for example, the Netherlands, where being blunt towards others is seen as a sign of friendship and honesty.

An example – the Dutch language has the expression 'Being straight through the sea', meaning to express 'no diversions', and describing directness as a virtue. At Amsterdam Airport, the announcement made for the last passengers to board their plane is 'Will last remaining passengers please go directly to the gate or we will proceed to offload your luggage'.

'High context' communication is, in contrast, a way of expressing oneself where the message lies in the (sometimes invisible) context informing the words, rather than in the words themselves. In high context cultures, it is thus up to the listener to interpret the message by paying attention to subtle clues such as the tone of voice used, the timing of a communication, who else is present, the type of room in which communication takes place, pauses and silences, and so on.

If that may sound like a bit of a minefield to the uninitiated (from low context cultures), it probably is. In her book about working as Secretary in a Japanese company, Belgian author Amelie Nothomb writes humorously about her series of professional demotions due to a failure to pick up the invisible and unspoken clues in professional communication. As a result of this failure her career path plunges from executive secretary to lavatory attendant.

What Nothomb really tells us, with considerable irony and humour, is that reading between the lines is a key feature of Japanese communication style. The Japanese do not say much, but the recipient understands 10 times more than what is said, based on 3000 years of continuous refinement of communication, and thus now requiring deep insight and experience to achieve for the modern non-native Japanese speaker.

In the diagramme below, we show how a range of countries fit within the 'high' and 'low' context culture dimension of cultural difference.

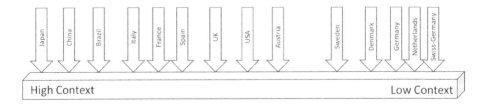

Managing differences between direct and indirect communication in virtual facilitation

This kind of complexity of context suggests that, when leading a virtual meeting, it is vital to manage any differences in directness of communication. According to Worldwork ('World of difference' film), people from high context cultures (indirect communication) may be perceived by those from low context cultures as 'confusing, unreliable, dishonest, insincere, uncritical, time-wasters'. Conversely, 'direct communicators' may be seen as 'cold, untrusting, insensitive, destructive of relationships...' by those who are more indirect by nature.

As virtual facilitators we notice the very positive difference it makes to the atmosphere and mood of any virtual meeting when people try to take care of their cultural differences with sensitivity and respect. In the textbox are two anecdotes to illustrate the point.

DUTCH AND BRITISH MISUNDERSTANDING

In a recent virtual training session, a Dutch participant (low context culture) gave some blunt but well-intended feedback to the British (higher context culture) facilitator who, slightly taken aback, paused for a second while thinking how to respond. The Dutch participant, hearing the pause, instantly recognised that he may have been a little too unsubtle in the message, and said swiftly: 'But I understand that I may have said that too directly for your comfort, excuse me please'. The point here being that open reflection on cultural difference can sometimes ease the way (as it did here) to improved understandings of difference and thus enhanced relationships.

CHINESE AND FRENCH 'AHA' MOMENT

Working with a virtual training group of corporate participants from China and France, we explored their differences on this dimension by providing feedback to each other. The French delegates saw themselves as very relationship-focused and caring, but heard from their Chinese counterparts that they found the French extremely task and results-focused, paying little attention to the relationships within the group, and regularly causing offence to their Chinese colleagues. The self-image of the Chinese participants, which was based on their sense of themselves as entirely clear and transparent in communication, was in turn rocked by the view of their French colleagues that they came across as fuzzy and enigmatic in their communication style. The session proved a real 'Aha experience' for both cultures, and slowly the group started to develop a 'third culture', based upon the needs and values of both.

From these two examples, we can see that the leader of any virtual meeting or training session can encourage mutual understanding by making the differences explicit and inviting the group to develop its own 'language', balancing transparency in communication with the need to preserve harmony and protect relationships. In the **Resources** section at the end of this book, there is a sample email text illustrating the balance between those two factors.

Dimension Two – Hierarchical or Egalitarian?

The second dimension of cultural differences that you need to be aware of as a virtual communicator is that of the 'social hierarchy', which in some cultures is viewed as flat and unimportant, and in others steep and meaningful.

So what is social hierarchy and what does it suggest about national culture? One distinction is that in egalitarian cultures, the notion of equality is seen as a virtue. Sweden is regarded as having a 'flat hierarchy' and this is reflected in the Swedish language by the word 'jämlikhet'. 'Jämlikhet' translates as 'being equal' and it is a guiding principle in Swedish society, where children are taught to see others as equal to themselves. The polite form of 'ni' ('vous' in French) was virtually abolished in the 1970s and most people are addressed with 'du'. Another reflection of this notion of equality is the taxation system in Sweden – whereby high taxes indicate that wealth should be distributed equally, to minimise the gap between rich and poor.

In egalitarian cultures generally, children are encouraged to develop their own opinions and it is seen as positive to challenge one's parents and teacher. Similarly, workplace employees will openly disagree with their boss, who actively expects and appreciates this kind of positive dissent.

In cultures where the hierarchy is described as steep, on the other hand, respect for seniority is a guiding principle. Children are expected to show respect, even reverence for, and obedience to their parents and teachers, and not to openly challenge them in public or private. In the workplace, the opinion of the superior is also not challenged or questioned in public and disagreement may be expressed in a more indirect way, behind the scenes, rather than directly to the person concerned.

						Russia	Saudi Arabia
Netherlands			USA				
Denmark				Germany	Mexico		Japan
Sweden		Israel	Canada			China	
			UK	Brazil	Poland	India	Korea

Egalitarian	Australia	Finland			Spain	Turkey	Peru	**Hierarchical**
		Austria			France			Nigeria
					Italy			

'Hierarchical or Egalitarian?' (Meyer 2014)

Managing the differences between hierarchical or egalitarian cultures

As you might imagine, some of these differences in hierarchical structure play out in various ways when communicating and working virtually. Here are some examples of that.

When expressing disagreement to seniors and 'the boss', it is likely that the 'hierarchy effect' will show itself in various ways, one of those being the degree to which participants will follow their own initiative (eg not 'just' politely following instructions from the meeting facilitator, trainer or coach) and also the extent to which they will show disagreement or resistance openly, or not.

Thus, for example, if the participants' boss is in the session, those from hierarchical cultures will tend to speak only when invited, and to not openly disagree with him or her. Those from egalitarian cultures, in contrast, are likely to feel less constraint about speaking up and telling the senior in the group what their opinion is, even if it is controversial.

Another point that distinguishes cultures with steep or flat hierarchies relates to the expectations that participants from those varying cultures have of the purpose of the meeting itself. This is particularly important in our experience, because when assumptions about what the meeting is for are not properly explored and agreed in advance, this may lead to misunderstanding and irritable feelings.

For example, participants from France (relatively hierarchical) may expect that the meeting is to announce a decision that has been made before the meeting, whereas a North American expects the decision to be made in the meeting (relatively egalitarian). The Arab participants might expect the meeting to be a ritual used to strengthen trust in the group (relationship focus). How to deal with these important differences? If you are leading or facilitating a virtual meeting or event with participants likely to represent these kinds of cultural differences, first think clearly what the purpose of the meeting is and how to communicate this to all participants. You will also need to be aware of different levels of seniority in the group you are working with, and think of how to reconcile the need to show respect with the need to move forward and get the job done.

In the textbox is an example to help you consider how to manage 'hierarchy in action'.

A few years ago we worked with a geographically dispersed team, with members from Hong Kong and from the US West Coast. While talking to the US team manager before the team coaching sessions, she mentioned the challenge of getting the Chinese team members to contribute as much as the American members. The view expressed by the American team members of their Chinese counterparts in this group was that they 'do not speak up enough during virtual meetings' – in particular, the Americans noted, when the boss is present.

We also heard from the Chinese team members, who told us privately that: 'the Americans like to speak a lot during meetings. We just listen politely until the meeting is over and then get on with the job'.

A tricky difference of view. How would you deal with this as the facilitator?

What we did in this case was to:

- talk openly with the whole team together about cultural differences in communication styles and

- invite the team to discuss their information needs.

The whole team agreed that the boss would call on individuals specifically if she wanted input, rather than waiting for people to 'volunteer'. The team also agreed to use the chat box during the meeting, as the Chinese participants said it was more comfortable for them to use written communication; less invasive than speaking up in the meeting.

This is only one example with two very different cultures. No one way is likely to work in every situation, but we have learned that open discussion of cultural differences can be extremely helpful in increasing understanding of others' needs and expectations. It also invites us to look again at our own needs and expectations (and how our expectations may impact on others) when working in a diverse team.

Dimension Three – the Task or the Relationship, which comes first?

In all work settings, there is a subtle balance in focus going on for every single employee at almost every moment of the working day, whether or not we are aware of it, or understand its importance. And that is the balance between getting on with the assigned task we are undertaking, or managing the relationships which may help to make that task easier, or even possible. And of course much of the time we may be doing both, without realising it.

In order to work together, people first need to make a connection or relationship. This is universal – if we work with others, whether in close proximity or otherwise, we will need to a greater or less extent to get to know them a little, to communicate with them, to try to understand what matters and does not matter to them in their working lives. And build trust.

So far, so good. But the next step is different, depending on the culture we are in. People from the Arab world, for instance, tend to take a long time, sometimes years, to get to know their business partners much more deeply than people from other cultures might do, in order to build the relationship and establish a common ground of trust and reliability. Much happens before simply 'getting down to business'. Many a collaborative project has failed to materialise at a late stage of development because even though the contractual obligations had been carefully explored, the relationship between business partners had not been properly nourished or was not sufficiently long-standing and therefore judged unreliable. In such cultures, a person's word is extremely important, taking on a far

greater significance and value than the most tightly-worded and carefully signed contractual document.

In the graph below, the 'point of entry' is either the task, or the relationship – depending on your cultural beliefs and values.

Differences between 'task' and 'relationship'-focused cultures

So how might these differences of perspective show themselves in virtual meetings, web training sessions and so on? In a culture where building relationships is seen as of critical importance, for example, managers are likely to mistrust telephone coaching. The personal relationship, with its rituals of hospitality, is of such importance culturally-speaking that no real work can be done without it.

And, as the communication style tends to be indirect, negative feedback will not to be given explicitly, but communicated in an indirect manner instead, for instance by 'forgetting' to respond to emails. What this may mean is that participants in virtual meetings and other events from those cultures may be feeling uncomfortable with what can feel like an 'impersonal' way of working at first – and they may also, due to the preference for indirect communication, hold back in saying so explicitly.

Conversely, in task-focused cultures such as North America, the tendency is to get on with the work as soon as possible. Lengthy socializing is seen as wasteful and unnecessary. This cultural understanding is exemplified through expressions such as 'let's roll up the sleeves', 'time is money' or 'let's get down to business'. Generally speaking, feedback is offered in fairly direct terms and viewed as valuable in enhancing collaborative working relationships.

These approaches, then, are almost entirely at variance, on this dimension of cultural difference at least. The North American 'frankness' may seem unfathomably rude, even humiliating to people from a culture – such as in many Arabic countries – where there is an important emphasis on carefully-cultivated relationships. To many Americans, the timeframe required to do business via social interactions may seem excessive, unproductive and sometimes entirely unwarranted.

How to manage these differences as a virtual meetings leader or facilitator? Here are some practical tips.

PRACTICAL TIPS

- **Take care to build relationships and 'virtual closeness'.** For participants from relationship-focused cultures, connecting in virtual space may at first seem foreign and distant. The task of the leader or trainer is to show and role-model relationship building in virtual sessions and build what we call 'virtual closeness'.

- **Invite some open discussion of differences early on.** If people start the meeting or sessions you are running with an understanding of each other's different perspectives, it is very helpful in cementing a productive relationship between all participants.

- **Be patient.** Cultural differences are not often swiftly understood and dealt with in one quick discussion. If you are running ongoing meetings and live events with a particular group or team, be ready to return to the topic.

- **Use the 'check in' process** to enable people to share their feelings as well as ideas and to help others connect with them at every meeting, whether it's a one-off or one of a series.

- **Encourage feedback** throughout your meeting or series of meetings. Even though direct feedback is not always easy for people, highlighting its value and purpose can help people get to know each other and share their feelings and views in an open and respectful way.

- **Bear in mind that there are challenges for people** in both task and relationship-focused cultures in working virtually. While it may initially feel more natural to work virtually for people from task-focused cultures – because their tendency to jump to the task quickly helps them to focus on what needs to be done – this may also mean that they 'get down to business' too quickly and overlook opportunities to build productive working relationships with other participants.

At the same time, while participants from relationship-focused cultures may at first fear that virtual meetings can make it difficult to really get to know and trust other participants, with encouragement and understanding, this view can change.

In the words of a previous participant in one of our training programmes (from a relationship-focused culture): 'I assumed before this (way of working) was cold and abstract, no connection possible; now I'm convinced of the opposite'.

Jean-Claude*, a French account manager for a large European high-tech conglomerate was assigned to the government account of a Middle Eastern country, for a multi-billion Euro contract. Month after month, he travelled to the capital to spend what seemed like hours and days drinking Arabic coffee and engaging in polite conversation. During his appraisal at the end of the year, his boss expected to see some results in the form of a signed contract. Jean-Claude pleaded for patience and was given another year to get the contract.

Following many more trips and countless meals and coffees, his clients asked lots of questions and made vague comments about the complexity of decision-making behind the scenes. The patience at HQ in France started running out and his seniors considered replacing Jean-Claude by another account executive. He explained that he felt a decision was on the way and after two and a half years of commuting he was awarded the lucrative contract. As a reward, Jean-Claude's division management gave him a promotion to country manager in Latin America.

However – much to everyone's surprise at HQ, the Arabs cancelled the order and turned out to be highly offended. After such a long time of building trust with Jean-Claude, he was gone and they were upset that they now had to deal with a new person. The contract as a legal document had no value. Obviously, Jean-Claude had to be repatriated from Chile and brought back to the Middle East to supervise the delivery of the contract.

(*the name has been changed to protect anonymity)

Dimension Four – Time: Do you see it as linear or cyclical?

'Time is on my side', according to the famous song by the Rolling Stones. But what side is that? How do you feel about time? Is it important for you to show respect by being prompt and precise, or do you respect others by being flexible about beginnings and endings? The first mindset we refer to as linear and the second one as a cyclical perception of time. In cyclical cultures, time is seen as abundant and multi-tasking prevails. In linear cultures, time is seen as a limited resource and something that needs to be managed. Here, people generally prefer to do one task at a time.

Beliefs about what time represents are often deep-seated and strong emotions are connected with them. Consider a Swedish family member who showed interest in my work as an inter-culturalist and questioned me about what I do. I replied that one thing I do is teach people about cultural differences in business, and, as an example of this, said that how people view time is an important cultural differentiator.

While listening to me, I noticed my relative's body stiffen and she looked very serious. I asked her what was the matter, and she said: 'There is only one way of dealing with time, and that is to be punctual. To be even a minute late is disrespectful and totally unacceptable, that would lead to chaos'.

To this family member, punctuality was such an important mark of respect, that she showed physical signs of distress purely by considering the notion that it might be possible to ignore deadlines and other time commitments in some cultures. And, from a Scandinavian perspective, punctuality is indeed key. In training programmes, Scandinavian managers tend to sit silently with their coffee cups in the training room at 08.25, ready for the 08.30 start.

At the other end of the spectrum, in the Arab world, respect is shown by honouring relationships, not the clock. To break off a conversation with an elder or superior in order to arrive on time at a meeting is seen as highly impolite. As a trainer in an Arab country, I am prepared that some participants will arrive early in order to have a leisurely coffee with me, while others will arrive late because they bumped into a friend or business colleague while on the way in. During the session, they will leave the mobile phone on, so that the boss or family members can reach them at any time, no excuses. This shows another difference between those from a linear and those from a cyclical culture with regard to time.

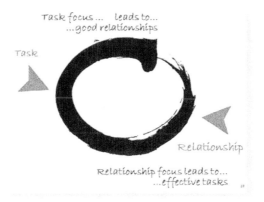

Task focus... leads to...
...good relationships

Task

Relationship

Relationship focus leads to...
...effective tasks

Getting time on your side as a virtual facilitator

So what does this mean for virtual facilitators in diverse cultural groups? Given the fact that virtual meetings are best kept short – since participants' attention span when sitting behind a computer screen is normally limited – time is, already, a scarce resource.

As many cultures with a cyclical concept of time also tend to be relationship-focused, it's extremely important to make sure this focus is honoured in the session itself. This may be done in several ways.

PRACTICAL TIPS

- **Making contact with individuals in advance:** In a continuing series of training events, for example, where a group is working together over some months, some facilitators like to contact each group member individually in advance to introduce him/herself and to ask people what they are hoping for from the training programme. This kind of conversation is partly about managing expectations; it is also about building trust and the relationship around which the success of the training will rely in 'cyclical time' cultures.

- **Virtual Café:** Another idea we like to use with training participants (and which could also work well in project groups and team coaching settings) is that of the 'virtual café', a friendly, relaxed setting before the official meeting starts, where participants can connect with others. We prepare a slide encouraging an informal chat, much as people meet, converse and 'catch up' in a face to face training event around the coffee table.

- **Check In, Check Out:** Experience has shown us that, even in a group of participants from a 'linear time' culture who are also very task-oriented (see above!), it is essential to include a brief 'check in' process at the start of each meeting. We have mentioned this earlier in the book and emphasise again the high value of a small, shared 'personal moment' with the whole group. We also close meetings with a brief and inclusive 'Check Out', with each person in turn making a comment about something they are taking from the meeting, or an insight they have gained.

- **Establishing and respecting time boundaries:** If you, the facilitator, are from a 'cyclical time culture', you will gain respect from the more 'linear time' participants if you start and end the meeting on time. If you are from a 'linear time culture', you will gain your participants' commitment by not rigidly enforcing your rules on them and showing some flexibility and 'lightness' around them. This is not an easy balancing act, we fully acknowledge. Open discussion and sensitively-led negotiation with participants is very helpful.

Discussing and establishing 'group ground-rules'

As illustrated under the paragraph on directness of communication above, a high-performing virtual group has the capability to 'make their own rules', and this is likely to be a very important part of the group's bonding process if they are working together virtually over time. The virtual facilitator will also have his or her 'rules of play' or virtual etiquette to discuss with the group (see *Chapter Five* for more ideas on this). However, much can be open to discussion, so that the unwritten preferences of participants become visible and a unique set of ground rules, which bring together and honour different perspectives and values can be created.

Empathic listening, summarising and reflecting back carefully are all likely to be important skills for the virtual facilitator negotiating 'group rules' in this often delicate but highly important conversation.

Chicago based LCW, an institute for Diversity Training, was asked by a global client in agriculture to roll out a programme on Diversity and Inclusion in 5 different countries (2013). The client was headquartered in the US.

Although the training sessions took place face-to-face, this case clearly illustrates the challenges of designing an event for audiences from various countries. The trainer wisely suggested to the client to do a 'cultural translation' of the training design.

This 'translation' involved local trainers from the training provider's network in France, Italy, Russia, Sweden and Turkey, all of whom were asked to screen the training programme (which had been designed from a north American perspective) on 5 different aspects and suggest relevant adaptations to meet the needs of their home culture. The 5 aspects for evaluation were:

1. Content
2. Elements of diversity (e.g. gender, age, sexual preference, religion, culture)
3. Timing
4. Pedagogy
5. Course materials

Here are some of the most interesting findings from the trainers' evaluations.

▪ In Italy, in a case study relating to sexual preference, one of the characters (a department manager) was changed from female to male. The reason is that a judgmental attitude towards gay people in the Italian workplace is much less prevalent amongst women managers. Also, examples involving race were removed because the notion of white and black does not resonate with an Italian audience.

▪ In Russia, diversity and multi-culturalism are sensitive issues. Areas of diversity that are acceptable to discuss are: regional differences, gender, age, migrants and disability, although it is as unlikely to find Russian employees in a wheelchair as it is a challenge to get out of most apartment buildings in a wheelchair. LGBT (Lesbian, Gay, Bisexual and Transgender) is an untouchable topic and was left out of the training design.

▪ In Turkey, the LGBT case study was changed into a case about conservative religious versus secular employees, where one character is uncomfortable with a more religious person and religious symbols at the office.

▪ In Sweden, the trainer should approach the group with 'attentive informality', well-prepared but toning it down. The amount of lecturing in the design did not work with the Swedish cultural norm of participatory decision-making. It was adjusted to allow for more conversation and dialogue than in the North American version.

▪ In Turkey, training materials needed to be serious to look credible. Jokes and illustrations had to be removed. As for style of facilitation, the trainer is seen as an expert and is expected to lecture to the participants. Asking frequent questions to the group might be taken as a sign of ignorance.

▪ As for timing, the half day training programme was much too short by Italian standards; this might imply that it is 'light' or unimportant.

Further practical tips for virtual facilitators working across cultures

In many international teams, English is used as the working language because it is the common denominator. Communication problems are the rule more than the exception. Non-native speakers, who use English as a second, third or even fourth language, may hesitate to speak up when they are not sure about their choice of words. And contrary to common belief, native English speakers are often at a disadvantage too. They tend to use colloquialisms and expressions, and create confusion often without even realizing it.

Understanding and working with cross-cultural differences is of course a vast area of expertise and below, we've set out some of the basic rules that conference interpreters use when working with speakers. These can be very effectively applied in virtual meetings also (Taylor-Bouladon, 2007).

PRACTICAL TIPS

- **Be aware of different cultural needs regarding greetings and introductions.** For example, German and French participants will often use Mr. and Mrs. with family names, even when they know each other quite well. For Americans, among others, this is entirely uncommon and might be seen as excessively polite – first names are used immediately in almost any setting. The order of mentioning first and family names varies across cultures, so that we often don't know which is which. How to get around all this? You might ask people, in a small group at least, to say how they like to be addressed. This is also particularly useful if, as facilitator, you do not know how to pronounce their name and need to hear it aloud first!

- **Acquaint yourself with some of the values and ideas relevant to the cultures** that you are working with. Focus on what is 'not said' – as well as what is explicitly stated. Of course you may not have time for in-depth research into diverse cultural values, but knowing about some of the dimensions we've set out that establish cultural differences is a good starting point. Remember that in high context cultures, a huge amount is unsaid but nevertheless understood (see textbox).

A Japanese trainer we work with, for example, talks about how 'reading between the lines' is really an important feature of Japanese communication style (Araki, 2014). 'We do not say much' he tells us, 'but the person receiving the message understands ten times more than what is actually stated.' Based on the importance in Japanese daily communication of the principles of harmony and living comfortably together without hurting other people's feelings, most Japanese people do not actually say 'No'. They may instead say 'let me think about it, I will come back to you'. If you have made a request of another person, and they say they will come back to you, but you get no further response – that really does mean 'No', even though you might never hear the word said aloud.

- **Be careful with your use of humour.** The truth is that sense of humour and what is deemed to be humorous are concepts which vary considerably according to cultural differences. Typically, humour does not travel well across borders and may create some confusion among participants. At worst, jokes and humorous comments made without sensitivity or consideration may be offensive to some and damage relationships.

  An example used in a training video on managing the cross-cultural project team highlights a British project manager who opens his first team meeting by saying 'they chose me to head up the project, for lack of a better person – ha ha'. This may be a typical example of self-effacing British humour intended with a degree of irony – to those who understand that. However, some team members from cultures who do not use self-effacing irony in that way may end up irritated – wondering why they got the second-rate project manager and who the first choice might have been *(Worldwork, 2012)*.

  It is quite possible that as participants in a group get to know each other, they come to understand this aspect of their cultural difference and accommodate, even enjoy it. However that is not a given, and at the start of a team process particularly, humour needs handling with care.

- **Be aware of grammatical and pronunciation differences** in language and the confusion they can create. As virtual facilitator it may also be good to realise that people speaking languages from other language families than one's own have totally different ways of expressing themselves. In Finnish for instance, there are no gender distinctions in the third person pronoun.

This means that a Finn or Hungarian tends to mix up 'he' and 'she' in other languages.

You do not need to be a linguist to appreciate and understand some of these distinctions; just knowing a few of these interesting grammatical differences can be helpful to avoid or clear up possible confusions when working in one language across cultures. Open discussion of some of these differences can also help, especially when you are working together as a virtual project team over time.

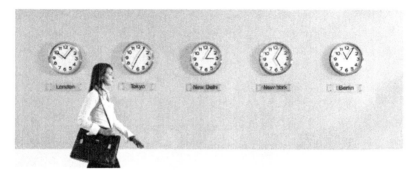

Intercultural competencies

Knowing the cultural dimensions described in the previous paragraphs is important for the virtual facilitator. On top of that, Brinkmann and van Weerdenburg (2014) set out four competencies that help us to be effective when working with an intercultural group in virtual space. These are set out here, with the key aspects of each included.

Intercultural sensitivity and awareness

This refers to the ability to see our own interpretations, norms and values as culture-specific and to consider other cultural perspectives as equally valid.

A key example of this might be the ability to pay attention to 'signals' – the extent to which we actively seek information about other's thoughts and feelings by paying attention to verbal and nonverbal signals when interacting with them.

Intercultural communication

This relates to the degree to which we actively monitor how we communicate with people from other cultures.

PRACTICAL TIPS

Two ways to achieve effective intercultural communication are by

- **Active listening:** Being mindful of how different values and perspectives affect how people understand each other when communicating across cultures, and paying full attention to others' expectations and needs.

- **Adjusting our communication style**: Our willingness and ability to adjust how we communicate with others in order to fine tune a message in line with cultural requirements.

Building commitment

This is about the degree to which we actively try to influence our social environment, based on a wish to build relationships and integrate people, and their needs and concerns.

PRACTICAL TIPS

We can actively build commitment by

- **Building relationships**: Investing time and energy in proactively developing relationships and diverse networks of contacts.

- **Reconciling stakeholder needs:** Seeking to understand the interests of different stakeholders, and creating solutions to meet these needs.

Managing uncertainty – by exploring our own fears and concerns, and those of others with openness and sensitivity.
This includes the degree to which we are willing to explore, and deal with the added complexity of culturally diverse environments.

PRACTICAL TIP

- **Exploring new approaches:** Be stimulated by diversity as a source of learning, risk experimentation, and actively try out new ideas.

The cross-cultural virtual facilitator

In general, the task of the virtual facilitator working cross-culturally is to navigate the linguistic differences and create a common, neutral language that helps people to communicate, minimises misunderstanding and is not offensive to anyone in the group.

That is an excellent starting point, and to achieve it you'll already be aware that knowledge of key cultural differences, self-awareness, enthusiasm, sensitivity and practice will help you considerably, just as these things do in face to face communication. You may also be feeling a bit daunted after reading this chapter – this is such a broad subject that communicating cross-culturally with effectiveness and sensitivity can at first seem like an insurmountable task.

However, working smoothly and competently with culturally-mixed groups and teams is entirely possible, even for the virtual novice. Starting with some practical insights and tips to guide you can help a great deal, as will being constantly willing to learn from your mistakes and develop your skills further. In truth, working as a facilitator with intercultural groups is a double-edged sword: it adds a layer of complexity to one's work. On the other hand, it can be so deeply rewarding that it may be hard to go back to working with a mono-cultural audience.

It seems almost certain that virtual facilitators will increasingly be required to work inter-culturally, with groups of participants in locations across the globe. Combining virtual effectiveness with cross-cultural competence and experience will therefore become an even more crucial skillset in the years to come.

References

1) Araki, S. (2014). Verbatim comment
2) Brinkmann, U. and Weerdenburg, van O. (2014). Intercultural Readiness. Palgrave MacMillan
3) Caulat, G. (2012). Virtual Leadership. Libri Publishing
4) Hall, E. (1983). The Dance of Life. Anchor Books Doubleday
5) Hofstede, G. (1991). Cultures and Organizations. McGraw Hill
6) LCW Language and Culture (2013). Presentation at Sietar Europe conference in Estonia
7) Meyer, E. (2014). The Culture Map. Public Affairs
8) Nothomb, A. (1999). Stupeur et Tremblements. Éditions Albin Michel
9) Taylor-Bouladon, V. (2007). Conference Interpreting. Booksurge Publishing
10) Trompenaars, F. (1997). Riding the Waves of Culture. The Economist
11) Worldwork (2012). World of Difference (training film). www.worldwork.biz

WORKING VIRTUALLY AND ORGANISATIONAL CHANGE | 9

By Hans Smit

Introduction

In this chapter we focus on working virtually from an organisational change perspective. As research and experience over the last decades tells us, changing the behaviour of individuals, groups or an entire organisation is one of the toughest challenges that exist and has a high risk of failure.

Many books have been written on this subject, using a large variety of models and perspectives that all have their merit in tackling change. They provide us with a framework to address change initiatives and enhance the likelihood of meeting our business goals, within the set timeframe and budget, and with the cooperation of a motivated and willing workforce.

Introducing virtual working as a change initiative in itself

In this light, implementing virtual cooperation in an organisation can be seen as a change project in itself. Despite its increasing prevalence and clear benefits in many cases, working remotely is often experienced as 'unnatural' or as something that is not suitable for the business environment people work in. Perhaps as a result of this, leading virtually is still something towards which many managers feel resistant.

The question then arises: how can we benefit from all the insights that organisational change research and practice provides us with, to enable this new way of working and to help us manage employees remotely?

Introducing virtual working as part of wider organisational change

Making the transition to remote working can also be part of a wider organisational change programme that aims to change the culture and established ways of working. The ultimate purpose usually involves achieving (new) business goals, decreasing cost, or (re)focusing on new products and services.

Working virtually can then be seen as one of the enablers of the new, or renewed, organisation that has to change more profoundly. New ways of collaboration are being introduced, together with new forms of leadership, and changes in the accountability, values systems and attitudes of the organisation's members.

The question then stands out: how can virtual training help to attract people towards this new way of remote working by reflecting the desirable reality of a renewed organisation with enhanced collaboration, leadership and accountability?

In this chapter we explore both these two concepts:

- Introducing virtual or remote working as a change initiative in itself

- Introducing virtual or remote working as part of wider programme of organisational change

But before we do that, we will provide a brief overview of one specific model that categorises and interprets organisations and their culture, which we will use as our framework and that will help us in answering these questions. We have chosen to use the Insights Model for diagnosing organisational culture as it is a simple yet powerful instrument; however we should emphasise that we could have chosen many other models to get a 'methodical grip' on this subject.

Finally, we will end this chapter with a generic checklist of contributors to success of organisational change and a list of typical obstacles and recipes for failure.

The Insights Model for diagnosing Organisational Culture
(Lothian, 2006)

Corporate Culture Model

This model can provide powerful information about organisational culture and behaviours, as well as its alignment with values, goals, capabilities and strategy.

Note that a specific personality type does not need to be unique for an entire organisation. Although most organisations can be typified by one dominant personality type, different dominant types can be valid for various parts of the organisation such as divisions, business units or countries.

These 'organisational forces', or organisational personality types, can be described as follows.

COOL BLUE | THE HIERARCHY CULTURE (CAMERON & QUINN, 1999)
Cultural characteristics

- Resistance to change
- Good internal coordination
- Traditional systems of governance, management and operation
- Process is more important than content
- Task-driven
- Strong internal orientation
- Stability and order are valued
- Analysis, information and control
- Direct control of staff
- Formal standards
- Closed communication which does not allow for expression of feelings, ideas, individuality or creativity.

This type of organisation can be described as a very formal and structured place to work. Procedures govern what people do. The leaders pride themselves on being good co-ordinators and organisers who are efficiency-minded. Maintaining a smooth-running organisation is most critical. Formal rules and policies hold the organisation together. The long-term concern is for stability and performance with efficient, smooth operations. Success is defined in terms of dependable delivery, smooth scheduling, and low cost. The management of employees is concerned with secure employment and predictability.

Typically, 'cool blue' organisations can be found in highly operational environments such as the military, logistics or manufacturing sectors.

EARTH GREEN | THE CLAN CULTURE (CAMERON & QUINN, 1999)
Cultural characteristics

- Avoiding change
- Interdependent relationships
- Informal standards
- Emphasis on people and teamwork
- Decisions by consensus
- Internal group orientation
- Loyalty and commitment to the group is highly valued
- Harmony and group cohesion are seen as important
- Indirect control of staff.

This type of organisation can be described as a very friendly place to work, where people share a lot about themselves. It operates like an extended family. The leaders, or heads of the organisation, are considered to be mentors and perhaps even parent figures. The organisation is held together by loyalty and tradition. Commitment is high. The organisation emphasises the long-term benefit of human resources development and attaches great importance to cohesion and morale. Success is defined in terms of sensitivity to customers and concern for people. The organisation places a premium on teamwork, participation and consensus.

**SUNSHINE YELLOW | THE 'AD-HOCRACY' CULTURE
(CAMERON & QUINN, 1999)
Cultural characteristics**

- Embracing change
- Creativity and innovation abounds
- Indirect control of staff
- A focus on hypotheses
- Risk-taking
- Proactive orientation
- Informal standards, open communication
- Quick to build relationships
- Inspiration and entrepreneurship are rewarded.

This type of organisation can be described as a dynamic, entrepreneurial, and a creative place to work. People stick their necks out and take risks. The leaders are considered innovators and risk-takers. The glue that holds the organisation together is commitment to experimentation and innovation. The emphasis is on growth and acquiring new resources. Success means gaining unique and new products or services. Being a product or service leader is important. The organisation encourages individual initiative and freedom.

**FIERY RED | THE MARKET CULTURE (CAMERON & QUINN, 1999)
Cultural characteristics**

- Accepting change
- Emphasis on action
- Goal directed, results count
- High responsiveness
- Striving for continuous improvement
- Productivity valued
- Direct control of staff
- Externally focused
- Speedy implementation.

This type of organisation can be described as result-oriented where the major concern is getting the job done. People are likely to be competitive and goal-oriented. Leaders are hard-driving, productive and competitive. They are tough and demanding. The glue that holds the organisation together is an emphasis on winning. Reputation and success are common concerns. The long-term focus is on competitive action and achievement of measurable goals and targets. Success is defined in terms of market share and penetration. Competitive pricing and market leadership are important.

Introducing virtual or remote working as a change initiative in itself

In our experience, supporting managers and professionals in organisations to become effective at learning and working remotely is more than just about helping them to acquire new skills. It can be defined as a change project where several elements in the 'system' need to be addressed in order to accomplish the desired outcomes for individual learners and leaders.

As soon as we are able to classify organisations in terms of their dominant culture (perhaps following the model suggested above, or another like it), we can ask ourselves if a certain organisational culture is able to adopt and learn the concepts of virtual collaboration more easily than organisations with a different cultural 'energy'.

As we have seen when describing the 4 different cultural types, organisations with a hierarchical (Cool Blue) and with a clan (Earth Green) culture tend to have difficulty embracing any type of change, either resisting or avoiding it. When dealing with these types of organisations, for example, special care should be given to introduce this new way of working and managing. For specific tips, we refer to the success factors and pitfalls of organisational change at the end of this chapter.

Introducing change in these types of organisations will take more time and encounter more resistance, criticism and either formal or informal obstacles than in those of the other types of culture. Thus, great attention should be given to communicating proactively, actively involving employees and staff, achieving change 'sponsors' at management level, and establishing a transparent implementation process with clear milestones and room for feedback and adjustments.

As approaches to virtual working are very diverse and can look quite different from one organisation to another, it is important that the 'new way of working' in any organisation is implemented with respect and sensitivity, aligning closely with the dominant values and belief system of the organisation itself. The implementation approach should reflect, confirm and emphasise these core organisational values and beliefs in order to minimise the degree of change experienced by individuals and teams within it.

Here are some examples of what this could look like.

Cool Blue | The Hierarchy Culture

Note that in this type of organisation the task is more important then the relationships between people. Structures and procedures bind people together. It is important that virtual collaboration technology supports and reflects that.

PRACTICAL SUGGESTIONS

- Preferably use only proven and known technologies

- New collaboration tools should be 'no-nonsense' and tried and tested thoroughly, removing all bugs

- Implement new tools gradually, step by step and only when necessary – as the saying goes, 'if it ain't broke, don't fix it'

- Offer (extensive) training and support via a helpdesk

- Prepare well for use of new tools and techniques and offer support in virtual meetings; such as a meeting producer

- Run virtual meetings in a disciplined manner, with a clear agenda, objectives and time schedule

- Avoid surprises and build in predictable ways of working

- Limit the opportunities for spontaneity

- Allow shared group files for project (status) information and exchange of working procedures

- Introduce a workflow management system (WfMS) as collaboration tool.

A workflow management system (WfMS) is a collaborative software system for the set-up, performance and monitoring of a defined sequence of tasks, arranged as a workflow.

Workflow management systems allow the user to define different workflows for different types of jobs or processes. For example, in a manufacturing setting, a design document might be automatically routed from designer to a technical director to the production engineer. At each stage in the workflow, one individual or group is responsible for a specific task. Once the task is complete, the workflow software ensures that the individuals responsible for the next task are notified and receive the data they need to execute their stage of the process.

Workflows can also have more complex dependencies; for example if a document is to be translated into several languages, a translation manager could select the languages and each selection would then be activated as a work order form for a different translator. Only when all the translators have completed their respective tasks would the next task in the process be activated.

Earth green | The Clan Culture
Note that in this type of organisation trust and the relationships between its members are key factors on which the organisation thrives. When collaborating virtually, special attention should be given to this to ensure that these important needs of employees are fulfilled. The way in which the virtual environment is arranged should provide for this 'virtual closeness'.

PRACTICAL SUGGESTIONS

- Face to face contact plays an important role

- When designing and implementing virtual collaboration, involvement of employees is important. A participative approach is recommended

- Use high touch technology such as webcams, video conferencing and Tele-Presence technology (See: 'Social presence', **Chapter Two**)

- Involve team members in building the agenda for virtual meetings

- Schedule ample time for check-in and check-out during virtual meetings

- Set an appreciative climate, recognising each individual's contribution

- Make ample use of chat functionality

- Managers should have frequent synchronous and asynchronous contact with reports

- A coaching style of leadership fits with this type of culture.

As we have seen, organisations that can be typified by the 'ad-hocracy' culture (Sunshine Yellow) or market culture (Fiery Red) can be expected to embrace or at least accept change. But as these organisations have a different type of 'organisational glue' – values, needs, motivators and definitions of success – they also have different demands when collaborating virtually.

Sunshine Yellow | The 'Ad-hocracy' Culture

Note that in this type of organisation, people tend to be self-managed to a high degree and intrinsically motivated. The manager's role could be described as 'herding cats'. Commitment and experimentation are the organisational glue. In this innovative environment where individual initiative, freedom and experimenting are encouraged, working remotely and virtually probably comes naturally and is likely to fit the organisation.

However, a pitfall here can be that working virtually reinforces the divergent character of the organisation, where there is an abundance of new ideas and initiatives with few clear choices being made or projects completed.

Implementation of a virtual working environment therefore should provide processes for bringing together different ideas and initiatives, rather than making 'fragmentation' more likely. At the same time, the processes used need to fulfil the needs of the individual employees.

PRACTICAL SUGGESTIONS

- Provide a variety of communication tools
- Use interactive technology such as web meeting platforms, mixing many different features
- Use new forms of groupware
- Avoid using webinars, teleconferences and videoconferences that are dominated by monologues
- Experiment with new tools and techniques
- Have groups of employees try new tools and techniques
- Make use of trial subscriptions and beta-versions of new technology
- During meetings apply a loose structure with ample room for experimentation and errors
- Be flexible with agendas
- Make ample use of images and video as opposed to text
- Work with self-steering teams without a fixed chairperson
- Evaluate often; at the end of meetings and projects; for instance by using polls at the end of a session
- Apply a participative management style and give team members freedom
- Manage performance by defining outcomes, rather than focusing on the input of individuals.

Fiery Red | The Market Culture

This describes a highly competitive, goal-driven, externally-focused, and action-oriented type of organisation with direct control of staff. Here, people tend to strive for (individual) success and aim for a high degree of efficiency. Although the organisation is willing to accept change, working virtually in this environment can be a challenge.

Managers in this type of organisation might feel their need for direct control is not met when there is less face to face contact, and this issue must be addressed when introducing remote working. Another point to consider is the apparent contradiction between individuals being results-driven and at the same time extraverted, needing interaction with others.

As this type of organisation can be described as rational and efficiency-focused, the choice and use of technology will most likely be done in a smart way, using the best suited technology for the goal without wasting any time.

PRACTICAL SUGGESTIONS

- Face to face contact continues to play an important role
- Smart and rational use of technology; see task-technology matrix in *Chapter Two*
- Keep virtual meetings short, efficient and goal-focused
- Prepare well beforehand and set a clear agenda
- Distribute shared action lists after meetings
- Give attention to efficient handover of tasks and data between locations
- Train or coach managers in letting-go of direct control and shifting to a more indirect way of controlling
- Introduce a structured virtual performance management system (or other groupware application) to communicate and store targets and measurements of performance
- Use high-end video conferencing or Tele-Presence to satisfy the extraverted style that is likely to prevail.

Introducing virtual or remote working as part of a wider change initiative

In some cases implementing virtual collaboration is part of a larger organisational change process in which a change in the organisational culture is desired. Then, a boost of a different 'culture colour' may be required, to counterbalance the negative effects of the organisation's dominant culture.

We will give you some examples and ideas on how a specific cultural energy can be boosted when collaborating remotely. As this is relatively new terrain, these suggestions are based on our own experience as practitioners.

BOOST A TEAM'S USE OF COOL BLUE ENERGY

- Set up a structured group site for documenting and sharing project status information and concrete deliverables

- Introduce a Workflow Management System

- Use a portal to document and share team procedures; do's and don'ts

- Implement a virtual Management System with controls that include appropriate use of process, defined roles and a model for governance

- Share public action lists with ownership of results

- Provide room to consider all the angles before making team decisions

- When communicating, give much attention to facts and accuracy

- Approaching personal issues in a standardised and objective manner; e.g. evaluating performance, workload, applying diversity and decision-making processes.

BOOST A TEAM'S USE OF EARTH GREEN ENERGY

- Choose high-touch technology such as webcam, video conferencing and tele-presence tools

- Make room for personal checking in and out in each virtual meeting

- Allow interpersonal chat during virtual meetings

- Encourage managers to establish frequent asynchronous contact with employees

- Encourage team members to explore each other's individual talents and make use of those

- Acknowledge individuals' personal issues

- Support team action plans with a well-communicated set of team values

- Build in moments of reflection before making final decisions

- Involve the whole team in key discussions (making use of different types of virtual communication to accommodate individual preferences)

- Give attention to virtual closeness with friendly open relationships.

BOOST A TEAM'S USE OF SUNSHINE YELLOW ENERGY

- Look for creative ways for the team to express itself

- Respond positively to flexible new ways of working and collaborating remotely

- Create structures to help the team explore new possibilities and create new challenges; for instance via 'virtual brainstorm rooms'

- Encourage dialogue and use breakout sessions in order to make better group decisions

- Activate all features, including chat boxes and polls, with challenging propositions
- Involve (the view of) stakeholders in team decisions
- Use interactive technologies such as web meeting platforms that allow different (pro) active ways of communication
- Use pictures and video over text
- Create inspiring visions of the team's future with images and video.

BOOST A TEAM'S USE OF FIERY RED ENERGY

- Keep meetings short and goal/action focused
- Prepare well, set and share the agenda beforehand
- Introduce a shared structured virtual performance management system
- Publish concrete action lists online with timelines and ownership details
- Share and involve current facts before decision-making
- Standardise procedures for dealing with personal issues
- Keep track of progress of actions (for instance with use of a shared digital dashboard) and celebrate/reward achievement of goals and results
- Monitor team efficiency digitally (time spent, costs, revenue, results etc.) and challenge individuals to come up with actions to improve
- Make rational use of different technologies according to the **Task-Technology Matrix** in *Chapter Two*.

Five Success Factors for organisational change

Effective sponsorship

Overwhelmingly, the greatest contributor to success in organisational change is executive sponsorship.

What do effective sponsors do? They:

- Communicate a clear understanding of the goals and objectives of the required changes, so that no misunderstandings exist about what needs to be achieved and what everyone's role is in the whole effort. They frequently communicate the vision, benefits and their expectations. They ask questions, listen, and take objections and obstacles seriously

- Provide budgets and open doors to solution to obstacles

- Show active and visible support, both privately and professionally, by making references in their communication, orally and in writing

- Ensure that the change programme remains a priority on the organisation's agenda by reminding their direct reports, and by frequently asking employees about their experience, obstacles, benefits and progress

- Demonstrate their commitment as a role model of change. In virtual meetings, they display role model behavior such as logging in a few minutes early to test technology, have excellent audio, are comfortable with basic features of the technology used, and generally stimulate interaction

- Provide compelling justification for why the change is happening. In the case of the 'group from hell' in **Chapter Seven,** the executive might share the business case of the competitive advantage of virtual teamwork. Also, (s)he shares success stories from within the organisation, such as a virtual team that created a new product or service, or exceeded expectations of an important client.

- Provide sufficient resources to be successful. As we have seen in the previous paragraph, any project without sufficient budget and other resources behind it, is a lame duck. It will fail to take off.

In the context of virtual facilitation, sponsorship means that the executives 'walk the talk' when it comes to effective virtual communication. They are role models in chairing virtual meetings, using communication technology and building relationships across distance. Also, they are explicit in stating that they expect their direct reports to do the same, and they should coach them in developing 'good virtual habits'.

Gaining buy-in from front-line managers and employees

Getting support for the change process from employees and managers who are impacted by a new way of working, is another crucial element.

This could mean – for instance – early involvement of staff and managers at all levels in the design and preparation of virtual training or events.

We often form a 'design team' with people from the target audience and make sure to include some 'sceptical voices' so we get everyone's arguments on the table. We take those arguments seriously and use them as starting points for creating designs. A survey is another efficient way to solicit input from the complete target audience, rather than a handful of representatives in the design team.

All of this helps to avoid getting negative responses from people who wish to complain, but not suggest any solutions for improvement, once the intervention is delivered. The critical notions provide important information about the whole target audience and the most critical participant in the design time often becomes an advocate of the programme or change, as (s)he moves through the process.

Exceptional team

The change management project team itself is a vital contributor to success when introducing culture change that includes remote learning or working in an organisation. The skills, expertise, experience and commitment of the team is really as critical as the team leadership, which needs to be not only effective, but also inspirational.

When a new way of working is introduced, many eyes are watching the project team and its efforts. The members are in the picture. This means that successes are magnified and failures are exaggerated.

CASE STUDY

CREATING A DEDICATED TEAM FOR CULTURE CHANGE

A UK telecom provider started a courageous journey of shifting from office-based working to a model of flex-working where employees can decide for themselves whether to come into the office or work from home, or another remote location. The main driver in this change was to reduce housing cost, something the main competitors had done before them. Office rents in central London were a major cost factor and moving to a smaller facility outside London without forcing employees to relocate was the chosen strategy.

In an early stage, a steering committee was formed with one board member plus the VPs of facilities, operations, HR and IT. In addition, the project team was put into place with a senior leader to head it up and representatives from the various employee divisions, as well as an external change management consultant and a union representative. The project team started with a 3 day off-site meeting to build the team and plan the project. The members were released from their normal duties and could devote themselves full-time as a committed team to this pivotal project.

The telecom project team described here used a variety of communication tools and channels to achieve their purposes. These included:

- Town hall meetings for all employees where the CEO kicked off the project, explaining its purpose, benefits and risks in a transparent and motivating manner

- Open discussions with senior managers from HR, operations, and ICT about all the details that would impact individual employees

- The project team also had its own website, newsletters and a hotline

- Project managers visited department meetings to hear and address concerns

- Training was organised to familiarise employees with the new way of working

- HR set up meetings with each employee to go over the legal and financial consequences of the transition from office-based to remote working.

Continuous, targeted communication and a well-planned approach

Communication is a key contributor to success. Effective communication is consistent, open and honest, targeted at the specific recipient and delivered through a variety of media. As you can see from the above case study, this team used a variety of methods to communicate their key messages in appropriate and effective ways.

There is no one way to communicate change. Remember, too, that people vary in how they like to 'receive the message'. To a certain extent, this relates to psychological preferences such as Introversion or Extraversion. Typically, Introverts like to read and digest news via written media, and need time to reflect upon what it means to them. Extraverts with more expressive tendencies often prefer to hear 'the word' in open conversation and debate, and do not necessarily need a lot of private reflection time to take it in.

No single communication channel can effectively meet all these varying needs over time; diversity, repetition and consistency of message (as far as humanly possible in a change process that may itself be changing over time) are key.

'Change Bandits' – advocates for success

If you are involved in a process of changing people's way of working from predominantly face to face to a more virtual approach, we suggest creating 'pockets of success' in the organisation via the introduction of what we call 'Change Bandits', or internal ambassadors for the new approach, usually a very effective way to advocate for change.

How to do this? Usually, appropriate 'change bandits' are people who have been involved early, seen how the change process can work well for the organisation, and are consequently keen and ready to introduce virtual working in training, presentation or events. Through such people, a 'buzz' around remote working can be created.

Nine times out of ten, the positive energy from 'change bandits' will be contagious, and hesitant people who have not quite bought in to the new initiative will start to become curious and motivated. Over time, these 'hesitant types' will start seeing the benefits of virtual working and communication, compared with face to face contact. In many cases they will even start asking for it!

Eventually, the new way of working will become rooted in the organisation. And then the possibility of achieving success is higher – the organisational culture is ready for a new approach, and so are the employees who work in that environment.

So far, so good. But introducing remote working within an overall culture change process requires a clear understanding of some of the pitfalls and factors that can derail even the most dedicated efforts. We list some of those here.

Pitfalls for organisational change and recipes for failure

Employee and staff resistance:

In many cases, employees involved in a process of culture change are fearful of the unknown and are opposed to moving outside of their comfort zone. This fear is often justified – after all, staff are dealing with something new and different that throws up challenges of individual skills development as well as technological adjustment, and a different kind of working atmosphere.

CASE STUDY
SHIFTING TO VIRTUAL TRAINING IN AN AIRLINE COMPANY

We have worked previously with the training department of an airline where the aim was to shift part of their internal training programmes for ticket agents, and sales and marketing staff from the traditional to the virtual classroom. One aim was to reduce the amount of travel that has to be done for training purposes. Often, staff are flown in from all corners of the world to attend 2 day training modules.

The virtual classroom is now used in this organisation to replace short modules so that all face to face training can be condensed into a single trip, supported by pre- and post programme virtual sessions. Some topics are even being trained completely virtually. Although some employees may appreciate having to travel less, other miss their bi-annual trip to head office, giving them a chance to connect with peers from other countries and spend the daily allowance shopping for items normally not available at home. Employees from cultures where hierarchy and status play a big role may feel sad to lose the status in their communities that the occasional trip to another continent brings. Some employees may fear that the cost-cutting aspect of virtual training is a forewarning of more reductions that may endanger their employment.

How to deal with resistance from employees who, as in the case study example above, may fear losing some of the benefits of face to face working, or be concerned that the switch to virtual training is a precursor to further cutbacks?

Coping with Employee Resistance

The key point here is that employees' fears need to be listened to, and acknowledged, not 'swept under the carpet'. Notably, the consultant introducing a 'virtual communication approach' into an organisation often hears, or hears of, plenty of what we call 'hallway conversations' – where people meet to gather and gossip. Quite often, these conversations perpetuate the idea that if employees remain quietly resistant and avoid the issue long enough, 'this too shall pass.'

However, if employees do not feel heard, they may express their resistance in an indirect or passive-aggressive way, by 'sabotaging' virtual sessions. For example, by logging on late, experiencing repeated technical problems, having to leave mid-session due to urgent issues such as the boss calling, and so on.

This type of resistance is not always expressed in a fully conscious manner, which makes it harder to deal with. We often 'forget' things for instance that do not suit our mood or interest, or that instil fear, without realising the true reason. In psycho-analytical terms this is referred to as a resistance mechanism, a way to avoid the painful emotions that may appear when facing reality.

Coping with Management Resistance

At other times, the resistance to change comes from managers as well as employees, and this can be for many reasons. They include fears about a perceived loss of power, and even loss of role, or simply not feeling fully involved and consulted in giving input into the change process.

As with employee resistance, any opposition, whether low-key and subtle or strong and explicit, is often not expressed directly to the consultant, or is only expressed indirectly via informal 'below-the-line' get-togethers and meetings. Managers clearly have considerable influence and are in a position to make a serious difference to how the change process plays out – so this can be a significant challenge for virtual facilitators.

A typical pitfall for trainers and facilitators is to jump into the delivery phase too quickly, rather than taking the time to explore the full context of the assignment. This should include surfacing the underlying hesitations, fears, power structure and hidden agendas.

Poor executive sponsorship

Executive 'sponsors' who either do not play a visible role in supporting the programme or shift their support too soon after project initiation, constitute another significant 'blocker' to progress in creating change.

To take an example – in the case of the 'group from hell' described in **Chapter Seven,** the initiative to train managers in working remotely came from Human Resources. Through benchmarking, HR had identified that the competition was clearly advanced when it comes to virtual working, and, alongside that, had appreciated that there is compelling evidence that being savvy at remote working brings a competitive advantage.

However, in this project, the executive level was not involved and continued to do 'business as usual', which involved mingling in the company's HQ coffee bar in the morning for relationship building and taking key decisions over lunch in the executive dining room. This behaviour clearly showed that the HQ coffee bar was 'the place to be' for those who wanted any type of influence, and those who tried working remotely positioned themselves way outside of the circles of influence and power. This is a clear-cut case of messages and actions not being coherent at a senior level within the organisation, with undermined the change effort quite significantly.

We learn from this example that

- Executive sponsorship needs to be active and obvious

- It should be visibly reinforced by leaders in their actions

- It needs clear, consistent role models – 'walking the talk' – for others to observe, be motivated and follow.

Limited time, budget and resources

This is perhaps one of the most common challenges. Teams that do not have adequate time to complete the change project are likely to represent one of the most important obstacles to the project's success. And, if resources are tight in any case, the additional strain caused by the impact of the change project only serves to compound the problem.

In these circumstances, teams struggling with restrictions of all kinds can be simply too burdened by their daily activities and responsibilities to engage with the change initiative. In this case, there is a negative impact on motivation: the project 'kick-off' generates energy and enthusiasm which is subsequently not honoured or tapped into. The result is that many people feel cheated and the more cynical voices in the company can rightly say 'I told you so; this is a waste of time and money!'

Corporate inertia and politics

Sometimes challenges facing introducing change to an organisation as a consultant, are presented not only by individuals or groups, but appear to come from every level within the organisation. In these circumstances, it's as if the organisational culture itself 'pushes back' against the change initiative.

This is not resistance that can be dealt with overnight. The good news is that there are ways of dealing with embedded, multi-layered resistance to change in organisations. The first step is recognising the challenges and the second is discussing them openly and devising strategies to overcome them.

When the facilitator or consultant picks up such strong signals of active or passive resistance, the best way forward may be to 're-contract' with the client. Any plan to quickly implement a new way of working should be postponed in favour of a thorough investigation of the current system, the purpose of the change and the full spectrum of resistance.

A final point about resistance to change

As numerous change management theories highlight, resistance and denial are practically inevitable, and might even be considered a healthy part of any change process. If, as a consultant or trainer introducing virtual communication into an organisation, by default you perceive employee resistance as a negative thing, something that should be sidestepped or 'overcome,' you miss opportunities to discover essential insights that might shift the change process into higher gear and help it along considerably.

SOME THINGS TO REMEMBER

- **Remember that you will almost always encounter some level of resistance** in complex change initiatives. It is a natural and usual human response to losing 'what is', not necessarily a bad thing.

- **Working with resistance competently** will always lead to better results than ignoring it

- **Find ways to work with resistance.** Seeking to 'overcome' resistance shown by others is likely to be counter-productive. Instead, find ways to work with it, and even ultimately benefit from it.

- **Deal with resistance in an open, positive way.** This is one of the most powerful methods to speed up the change process and make it more effective – thereby lowering its ultimate cost.

In our next and final chapter, we explore the future of virtual communication in more depth, looking at current trends and highlighting possible developments in remote working over the years to come.

References

1) Lothian, Andrew (2006). Transforming Individuals, Teams and Organisations.
2) Cameron and Quinn (2011). Diagnosing and Changing Organisational Culture, Jossey-Bass.

THE FUTURE – PUSHING THE BOUNDARIES

10

By Fredrik Fogelberg and Jude Tavanyar

"Everything that can be invented has been invented."

Attributed to Charles H. Duell, Commissioner, U.S. Office of Patents, 1899

It is a risky endeavour to write a chapter about the future of virtual facilitation. Many experts and great minds have made fools of themselves trying to make predictions for even the near future of what our lives will look like, and the role that technology plays in it. For instance, in 1977, Ken Olson, president and founder of Digital Equipment Corp., said there is no reason anyone would want a computer in their home. We typically predict what lies ahead through the lens of what has already happened, and what is going on now. Any chapter about the future is, by definition, a plunge into an entirely unknown world.

In this book we have looked at virtual communication from many angles and in this final chapter we put on our coloured spectacles – rose-tinted for optimism, but with a sun filter nevertheless, so that we do not dazzle ourselves 'blind' with too much enthusiasm. And we invite you to come with us and take a jump into the strange, ever-changing and uncertain world that lies ahead.

Before we do, let's highlight the purpose in doing so. Even if we can only envisage the future through the limited lens of what we already know and can imagine – 'through a glass darkly', in Shakespeare's phrase – it is worth the effort to look

'The Classroom of the Future' – Image from late 19th century

ahead because technological change is happening at such a pace that if we do not make some efforts to predict and prepare ourselves, it may, like a tsunami, sweep us up in its wake.

Trainers, coaches and consultants working through the technological revolution are aware that staying still is impossible. Not only is the technology changing, the 'rules' of communication are changing and the kinds of conversations we are now able to have with each other via diverse media in just a few seconds across thousands of miles may soon become so well-established and accepted that face to face presence for work becomes a laughably old-fashioned idea. By the end of their lives, if not before, our children may be astonished that people ever worked in the same room – some may even forget it ever happened.

So, looking ahead helps to remind us that we cannot now stay still. We cannot avoid living in a world where technology rules the day, and getting used to constant cycles of technological change and innovation is another given. It is also clear that this shapes our profession as coaches, trainers, facilitators and managers. That does not mean you have to change the technology you use every few months, but it does mean that you need to be constantly aware of the ways in which people are choosing to communicate professionally, and the demands of clients who are aware of these trends.

All that said, here are some of the questions we explore in this chapter.

- What are the current trends and some future possibilities in remote working and virtual communication?

- What might the remote workplace look like in a decade from now?

Current trends …

The evolving world of work

Lynda Gratton, professor at London Business School, has described the shift from traditional, office-based work to a new paradigm of working, in a number of stages, or, as she puts it, 'waves'. They are set out below.

Wave One: Virtual freelancers

In the mid-to late 1990s, freelancers were the first to begin using nascent Internet technologies to work from home. Over time came increasing opportunities to work with corporations remotely, even if not full-time. Gradually, the 'ecosystem' supporting virtual working began to develop.

Wave Two: Virtual corporate colleagues

In the first decade of this century, corporations began to allow full-time employees to work from home and started building virtual capabilities. British Telecom was among the first – not just to allow virtual work but to formally study its effects on productivity, employee satisfaction, and customer satisfaction. While productivity declined in the first year, it surpassed the normal levels in subsequent years. The performance of virtual workers was 20% higher on average, and their turnover 20% lower, than for onsite workers.

Employees loved the flexibility of remote work arrangements. Customer satisfaction also improved, as service was more available around the clock.

Wave Three: Virtual co-workers

The third wave is still playing out at the time of writing in 2015. Increasingly, virtual workers living near each other are leasing physical spaces to share – in other words, they are building 'hubs'.

In these hubs, people affiliated with different companies are working side by side, gaining the benefits of interacting and 'networking' with each other, and sharing resources. The formation of these 'work hubs' is a natural outgrowth of some of the challenges of virtual work. For example, young adults may not want to work from home, if they live in cramped quarters with room-mates. Similarly, freelance professionals might prefer to seek the company of like-minded people, rather than spend their working days at home alone and in front of the computer.

Future Possibilities

Surinamese-Dutch trend watcher Adjiedj Bakas makes predictions about the world of work in 2020. Some of the key themes he highlights include the 'nomadic' nature of virtual workers in the next 6 to 10 years, our portable lifestyle enabling us to carry our contacts and our work in our rucksacks, without an office base.

He also warns, however, that our desire to remain abreast of technological trends must not be at the expense of our own creativity. Finding the appropriate balance between enjoying the new possibilities of technology but not being overwhelmed by them is a tricky issue and, according to Bakas, generations to come will be much better at it than many of the readers of this book, whatever their age.

The professional, social and environmental revolution

Trite as it may be to highlight this, most people using computers from 10 to 35 years of age seem still to be more clued up, effective, confident and imaginative with technology in general than those in the – say – 50 years upwards age bracket. For this younger age group, says Bakas, technology is a 'given', a means towards shaping their lives as they want and using their talents to the full.

There may also be some serious reshuffling – and demise – of various job roles. According to Bakas, thrift and flexibility will continue to be the order of the day for the vast majority of the world's population. Indeed, Oxford economists predict that 47% of today's professions will disappear, including telemarketers, accountants and auditors. Computers are likely to replace all routine jobs, but for those active in bio-economics (using green supplies) IT security (cybercops) or entertainment and media, demand will very probably increase.

And just as the professional revolution occurs, so will the social revolution. Now that you can do almost anything you want over the Internet, we will see an increased number of people moving to the countryside. They simply will not need to be in close proximity to other colleagues to do their work. These shifts in location will result in the development of 'E-towns' with high-end Internet resources.

From an environmental perspective, we notice already that organisations seeking to seriously reduce their carbon footprint are already turning more to virtual communication and remote working, for that reason as much as for the important business case it makes. And hopefully, the ecological argument will speed up the move towards remote working. We note that at the time of writing the corporate giant Unilever is actively encouraging personnel to work from home and to use technology for meetings instead of flying people around the world, thereby greatly reducing its carbon footprint.

Perhaps the most obvious change we might anticipate is still worth mentioning here. For the many reasons we set out in this book generally it is absolutely apparent that the ongoing 'communication revolution' is an exhilarating and unstoppable one.

A change of attitude to working virtually

All that we can potentially control here as individual professionals working in virtual space is our attitude towards it. Writing the first version of this book in early 2015, we know that, in many organisations within which we work, the majority of managers and employees prefer face to face contact to virtual working, speaking of the 'coldness' of contact without visual, non-verbal cues. What they mean by 'coldness' may vary, but in many cases it is clear that after some time experimenting and getting used to working 'live' in virtual space, their position very often shifts and some even become quite evangelical about its possibilities!

We predict that over the coming years as people of all ages become more proficient and 'acclimatised' to the virtual communication world; we are likely to notice a change of attitude. We may well see a far stronger understanding and appreciation of the enormous possibilities of virtual communication to build trust, empathy and relationships in general.

We are also likely to see virtual synchronous communication – so to say – 'come out of the shadows' as a mere second best fall-back option to face to face connection, and take its rightful place in the minds of executives across the world as a highly valuable approach to communication in its own right. And that will involve a recognition that it is different from face to face communication, and not only equal to it in some ways but in others better, with its own rules and responsibilities, and the potential to inspire and stimulate people in ways that were previously considered impossible.

How technology is shaping our world for the better

In order to think about what may lie ahead in the most positive light, let's take a look now at some examples of communication technology already revolutionising society in 2014. The two cases described here, from agriculture and healthcare in Africa, highlight how communication technology is revolutionising the way people work in developing countries, and the enormous impact this has on how people in general communicate, teach, manage and facilitate.

A LEAP FORWARD IN EAST AFRICA THROUGH MOBILE TECHNOLOGY

African farmers' lives and livelihoods are transformed by mobile telephony and wireless technology services such as weather forecasts, agricultural extension services, commodity market information and mobile banking. Through mobile telephony, new business models can be developed that offer greater opportunities, reduce risks for smallholders, and help to meet the challenge of feeding an estimated 11 billion people by 2050.

HEALTH CARE AND EDUCATION

AMREF, also known as 'Flying Doctors', has built a Virtual Training School to provide nurses' training and professional development for health care professionals, located in remote and inaccessible locations. The school is becoming a virtual training centre of excellence for health workers in the Africa region. Success rates are high: students have registered a pass rate of 67%, considerably higher than the national pass rate from more traditional educational institutions (figures from amref.org).

The remote workplace in a decade from now

Each of the trends discussed above appears to suggest a kind of 'geographical dislocation' of company from worker, with all the upheaval and uncertainty that may bring in its wake. In many companies, that 'uncoupling' of employee from work location has already taken place, and while individual reactions to remote working may vary (depending on attitude to change, and communication preferences, among other factors) it is interesting to take a brief look at how some companies, and their employees, have responded to it.

Research into remote working – the Erasmus University survey

Erasmus University in Rotterdam, the Netherlands, conduct a survey of 300 organisations annually, to get a sense of how remote working is being managed and received by employees across these organisations. Remote working is defined variously in the Netherlands as both working from a remote location (such as at home, or in satellite offices) and also working in a 'flexible office', or office space where there are fewer desks than employees and no one has a personal desk.

What is interesting is that this particular survey shows recently that optimism for the 'remote working approach' may have declined somewhat in 2013. In 2012, 50% of respondents had a positive association with the concept, but this figure dropped to 39% in 2013.

Why is this? In the 2013 survey, the Dutch organisations questioned clarified five different benefits from the new way of working:

- Reduced cost for office space
- Increased employee satisfaction
- Improved work-life balance of employees
- More attractive employer 'brand'
- A more flexible organisation

However, of these expectations only about 25% are regarded as met, according to the survey. And of those that are met, most – such as cost reduction – are both measurable and can be seen to be achieved. The more abstract expectations – such as achieving a more flexible organisation – appear to be met less frequently.

The survey also suggests five obstacles that often get in the way when introducing remote working to an organisation. These are:

1. Fear of losing one's personal workspace
2. The organisational 'management style' does not fit remote working
3. Resistance to change from the management population
4. People fear losing contact with colleagues
5. Little 'fit' between organisational culture and remote working.

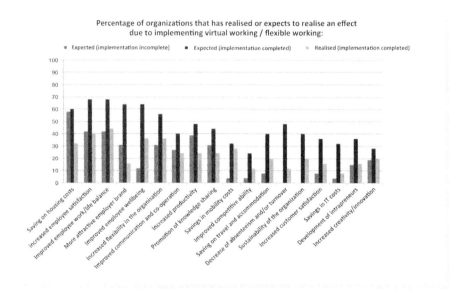

Percentage of organizations that has realised or expects to realise an effect due to implementing virtual working / flexible working:

While this study suggests that the virtual facilitator can play a role in helping organisations and its members to get to grips with 'the new approach', the Erasmus study also indicates that sometimes the leaders in any organisation can get in the way of this, acting as a major impediment to a smooth shift into remote working. This is because the revolution from collocated to remote working has particularly large consequences for managers and leaders. In the classic setting, their 'raison d'etre' was to control and monitor workers. In the new paradigm, they are asked to shift from a 'control' to a 'trust' modus operandi, and for many managers that is a difficult transition.

Is remote working stressful?

So what are the trends and general impact on individual remote employees that studies like the Erasmus Survey serve to elucidate? A key theme emerging in recent years is that the speed of change in our current world of virtual communication (itself increasing at an astonishing rate) is already having a detrimental effect on individual wellbeing in an increasing number of cases.

In our digitally-connected world, the kinds of communication that can trigger social and economic upheaval, or ruin the fortunes of the rich and famous, can be achieved in the time it takes to send out a series of Tweets. In this world, it looks as though almost anything is possible and achievable in a tiny fraction of the time it took human beings to invent a wheel.

These days, new concepts of speed apply, and nano-seconds count. We have become used to waiting less and less, and an additional second or two in a traffic queue, or to get your laptop running in the morning may now cause deep frustration and irritation. The engagement span of a human being is now measured in seconds, not minutes, and our ability to 'save time' by multi-tasking while 'waiting' for the tardy laptop to kick into life is notorious. And, in order to avoid sitting and waiting, we will turn to other tasks and distractions, if they are there for us.

At the same time, whilst our focus is increasingly scattered across multiple tasks, our professional presence is increasingly required around the clock. As anyone with a portable computer and a decent Internet connection can now (in theory) be available 24/7, the concepts of 'signing off' and 'personal time' are harder to defend. There is evidence to suggest that the possibility of constant connection does not necessarily make us happy and relaxed, but rather the opposite. It is not for nothing that courses in 'mindfulness' and 'being present' proliferate in our high-speed society, and stress management coaching is increasingly requested for executives on the edge of 'burn-out'. Whether we worship at the altar of technology, or prefer to see its dazzling diversity as something of a mixed blessing – the assumption that we ourselves can function, like robots, without food, sleep or a personal life for extended periods seems to be a dangerous premise indeed.

High presence, low sleep?

An annual poll done by the the National Sleep Foundation in the Unites States shows that the number of hours of sleep that Americans get has gradually decreased. Over the last decade, the poll indicates that a growing percentage of Americans is sleeping less than six hours a night, and the number of people who get eight or more hours is dwindling. Doctors warn about the effects of sleep deprivation, such as car accidents, depression, anxiety and cardiovascular problems. They recommend seven to eight hours a day. Sleep deprivation has been likened to chronic alcoholism in its effects upon the body's health. (nationalsleepfoundation.org)

Remote working and burnout

Whether or not the natural increase in remote working has actually caused a general rise in stress levels is entirely open to debate. A study by the Dutch government looking into the relationship between burnout and remote working (Echteld van, 2014) shows that most employees respond positively to remote working. The results indicate that employees who are able to engage in remote working suffer less from emotional exhaustion and are more dedicated to their work, which translates into greater enthusiasm for their work and less exhaustion.

One obvious explanation for this is that teleworking reduces commuting time and enables employees to structure their work in a flexible way. Workers may also be exposed to fewer stressors, such as interruptions by colleagues at work. Autonomy and the ability to regulate their own work are also associated with less emotional exhaustion and more dedication.

The researchers also found that measuring the results that remote employees achieve, rather than the amount of time input into any particular work task, reinforces the positive associations between access to teleworking and autonomy, and dedication to the work required.

As a virtual facilitator, helping people to become better at working remotely, it is important to remember that we have different personalities and that the degree to which people adapt to remote working differs widely. To put the positive results, reported in the previous paragraph, into perspective, one may keep in mind that individuals with a high need for structure tend not to benefit from the increased level of autonomy that remote working brings, due to the lack of clarity and increased uncertainty it can also bring with it (Slijkhuis 2012).

The 'Human Factor': more important than ever?

Without consideration of 'the human factor', it seems likely that we may become imprisoned by our own technological competence and skills and forget that competence to perform well remotely as a virtual trainer, coach or team leader requires

- emotional intelligence as well as technical proficiency in order to establish trust
- empathy and intuition as well as logic and reason to build relationships
- self-awareness to know our strengths and limits, and what we need to be at our most effective

- a longer-term view as well as short-term survival skills, to look ahead and invest time in developing our approach to meet emerging needs and trends.

Many of these competencies – EQ and empathy being two obvious examples – are not typically associated with robots, and for all of them we need a brain that is rested, nourished and high-functioning. So let us hang on to our humanity, flawed and imperfect as we may be, and avoid trying to turn ourselves into machines in order to manage the multiple demands upon our time that remote working may impose, if we allow it.

What might the remote workplace look like in a decade from now?

The concept of flexible working space

Back in 1995, management writer Charles Handy described the office of the future as a place quite likely to resemble a clubhouse: a place for meeting, eating and greeting with rooms reserved for particular activities, rather than for particular people (Charles Handy, 1995). In some ways this idea is an extension of the current trend for 'hot-desking' – where even desks and chairs are reassigned daily, depending on who requires to use them. So Handy's prediction, some 20 years down the line, is turning out to be very accurate, as the picture below illustrates.

The days of self-contained offices with your name and title on the door are (almost) over – matching short-term need against availability and suitability of space is the name of the game. Outside the office environment, we currently see this idea in the concept of the 'pop-up shop' where unleased space can be used for short-term rental as a temporary retail outlet, for example.

The idea of any particular space being available for multiple uses in the office environment is clearly mirrored in the virtual classroom environment, where although on any particular platform the technological possibilities will stay the same, the mood, 'flavour' and purpose of the virtual meeting or event is likely to be quite different from one day to the next.

The project team goes virtual

Handy also predicted that the future is about project-based working, rather more than focused on intact permanent teams working to an agreed remit, with a specific and predefined team structure. Indeed, he considers (Handy, 1993) that team and organisational structures in general will be far less hierarchical in nature, with fluid roles and interchangeability of leadership responsibilities as defined by the challenge at hand.

> *'Work', said a friend in Dresden, 'used to be a place one went to,*
> *not something one did.'*
> **(Charles Handy, The Empty Raincoat)**

These 'flatter', flexible teams will work more regularly across organisational boundaries than the 'fixed' teams the past, and, Handy considered, will require what is known as 'boundary-spanning leadership', as referred to by Ernst and Chrobot-Mason (Ernst and Chrobot-Mason, 2011). By this, the authors mean the ability to work cross-divisionally, cross-culturally and across organisations with confidence and skill.

At the time of writing, we notice already that while there are many intact, fixed teams working to a single team leader with a clearly defined and permanent role. The trend towards remote, project-based teams appears to be undeniable.

And virtual teams will play an ever larger role in our worlds of work. With the number of telecommuters in the U.S. alone expected to increase by 69% to nearly 5 million people by the year 2016, the ability to lead virtual teams successfully is already a critical leadership skill. But a study in MIT Sloan Management Review found that only 18 percent of 70 virtual business teams globally in the study actually achieved their goals, so there is work to be done for virtual facilitators.

Virtual Team Leadership – the future?

Remote leadership remains a relatively new discipline, and therefore any analysis of required skills and behaviours is still likely to be limited. However, certain competencies to cultivate, and mistakes to avoid, already stand out in the experience of those working regularly in this field, and we note them here.

Swift trust and 'letting go':

There is no doubt that leading across distance makes all kinds of leadership demands which do not arise in the same way when working in shared physical space. The first challenge for leaders making the transition from collocated to remote leadership is to be aware that they cannot exercise control in the same way as previously – to take a somewhat negative example, they can no longer manage performance by 'checking up' on team members to see what they are doing and how long they are spending doing it.

For many leaders, this is a significant test of their ability to adapt and to work from a position of trust – at least, until the particular employee demonstrates that they are not worthy of being trusted. In other words, to let go of control, and assume the best of each team member, may at times lead to disappointments, but it is just as likely to create an atmosphere of openness and transparency, where people know that they are valued and recognised from the start, without needing to show themselves worthy of that recognition first.

Starting from a position of trust is a leap of faith for many leaders, but it is a leap very well worth taking, for different reasons. Although technology will soon allow the remote manager to 'play detective' over the Internet and constantly ascertain whether her team members are doing what they said they would do, this clearly is not the way to go. A psychological argument for showing trust as a 'given' at the start of any online relationship is that, without trust, people do **not** give of their best. While some may appreciate the constant requests for virtual connection a 'hands on' manager may seek when working over distance – many others will not. These others may, indeed, feel irritated, undervalued, even severely undermined by their boss or team member's refusal to take them at their word and not keep 'checking up' on them at all times.

Measuring performance by output more than availability

Remote leaders – especially those who like to exert a high degree of control over their staff – may need to change the criteria they use to assess performance from team members when working across distance. In virtual space, it is no longer possible to know what your colleagues are doing at all times, and for many managers, this would not be desirable even when working face to face.

Consequently, choosing to evaluate team members' contribution according to their output, rather than their constant availability and attendance at teleconferences and online meetings, becomes a more valid measure of success in a relationship where continuous face to face contact is not possible (Cune and Fogelberg, 2011). According to these authors, trust is the core of the relationship between boss and employee in a remote situation: 'Trust is the glue that keeps it all together and technology is the lubricant that keeps everything spinning' (Clemons and Kroth, 2011).

And for many managers who have been successful because of their ability to oversee employees' activity constantly, this shift to 'rapid trust' without constant connection is a painful one at first. As one French senior manager in China said: 'All my career, I have been used to seeing my team members arrive in the office in the morning, and now I have no idea where they are and when they work. And I don't like it at all!'

Focus on relationship

A key challenge for remote leaders is to balance the task and the relationship. We have already talked about this in **Chapter Five**.

For some reason, managers tend to be more task-focused when working remotely than when they are leading a collocated team. According to Caulat, any virtual meeting where little or no attempt is made to build a relationship with team members is, in some way, a step on the way to failure for the team (Caulat, 2006).

This statement is summarised in the following graph:

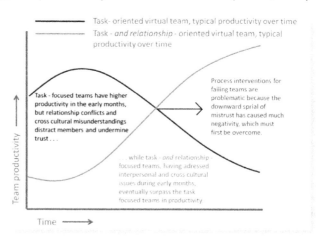

The role of the virtual facilitator: 'Facilitating people'?

But what do all the various developments portrayed so far in this chapter mean for virtual facilitators, whose profession it is to develop and teach, facilitate groups and learning processes?

In **Chapter Five**, we talk about virtual facilitation from many perspectives, and it is clear that the role is a broad one with many different skills involved. Simply keeping up with the latest technology is not, on its own, going to lead you towards success in virtual space. You will be tired of reading this by now: technology is only an enabler.

Compare it to learning how to drive: in a very short while, the novice gets used to the technology and then passes the test. After that, the driver can start enjoying the scenery, talking to fellow passengers or listening to music. The car becomes just a means, not an end in itself.

Similarly, when you buy a new smartphone, you need a few hours, days or weeks for some of us to fully grasp all features until it becomes your friend. Again, the device in itself is not what it's about, but all the possibilities that it offers. Nokia, once first in the world in mobile telephony and now almost extinct, used to be 'Connecting people'. I'd like to use that as a metaphor for what we do as virtual facilitators.

Facilitating people, whatever the technology is – that really is the 'raison d'etre' of any facilitator working across distance. There is no way to be proficient in all tools that appear on the market; that would be more than a full time job in itself as we see new technologies appear daily. For adolescents, email and text messaging are already seen as 'Stone Age'.

Facebook paid billions for Whatsapp in 2013 and already we are two generations of chat apps further down the line (Dagens Nyheter, 2014). According to research (Colman Parkes), we will see more and more high-tech in the workplace such as:

- Interactive surfaces, such as walls
- Voice recognition
- Augmented reality glasses
- Robots
- Drones

- Carrier nodes: ear devices that send electronic signals, such as Wifi, directly to the brain of an employee
- Videoconferencing – sending a hologram of yourself instead of attending personally
- Bluetooth for the brain.

Some of this technology may be relevant for our work in future, and some will not. I suggest we leave the training of how to use the technology to others and focus on the lasting principles of human development and interaction. These include learning theory, developmental psychology, group and team dynamics, psycho-pathology, ergonomics (man-machine interface), intercultural theory, negotiating, presenting, leadership, and basic skills such as listening, communicating and asking questions.

At a trainer's conference in the year 2000, one workshop presenter told us that in 10 years from now, the trainer in a meeting room with a flipchart and a set of markers, will be obsolete. I took that comment to heart and started exploring virtual facilitation. Seeing the number of trainers embarking on the journey of virtual facilitation, that shift is certainly taking place. The setting of our work as facilitators changes, the way people work may change as well as their motivation. But principles of human development and interaction remain.

Virtual presence: emerging rules, new responsibilities

As technology changes, so do the 'rules' of communication that derive from it, and from our growing expectations of quicker but still meaningful conversations across distance, of making friends with people we have never seen and may never get to see, of the possibility of being both powerful and anonymous at the same time – influencing and shaping lives through our (often invisible) presence via social media and other online channels.

Nowadays, being present in virtual space may have little to do with 'seeing, and being seen' as a real, live human being in the flesh, as it used to in public space. It may be more closely connected with factors such as the messages we choose to convey about ourselves, the kind of image we seek to present to the world through our marketing materials, the intonations and energy of our voice across Internet telephony, and the way we use social media opportunities such as Facebook and Twitter.

This freedom to be present without being tangible, or even visible, carries with it some critical considerations. It is not for nothing that we see now (EGS) almost daily another case of 'cyber bullying' via a malicious comment, say, on Twitter, or what amounts to serious and protracted harassment on Facebook via repeated inappropriate or abusive posts on other people's pages. We can still say almost anything to another person in virtual space and not be accountable for it, it seems, as the new 'rules of play' in respectful virtual communication are still tentative and unclear, and the legal framework to prevent intrusive behaviour still emergent with every new case that comes to light.

Another aspect that we need to take into account is the threat to our privacy, both from the side of national governments and from cyber criminals. Today, we have only seen the beginning of what both of these might imply. As virtual facilitators, we have a responsibility to protect the integrity and privacy of our clients and participants. This challenge is too overwhelming to solve as individual professionals but we cannot ignore this reality.

At the time of writing, a new play in the UK – 'The Nether' – portrays a world set in the year 2050, some 35 years after the first edition of this book was published. In this detached and chilly feeling universe, Internet connection (renamed 'the Nether') offers a vast playground of the senses where people may sign up and spend their entire lives as different personae, doing exactly as they wish to others with no legal redress of any kind, even opting in more extreme cases to ignore the 'real' world altogether, and spend their time in cyber space on a life support machine. In this way, they are able to remain physically alive but totally disconnected from real human contact, in some sense 'dead' to the 'real world' around them.

One of the most interesting themes of this play is the increasingly tenuous and confusing boundary between 'real' and 'virtually real'. While computer gaming increasingly dominates, creating dizzyingly innovative and sometimes stark and violent 'alternative realities', we still know where our 'real life' stops and what is 'digital playspace'. (Although, some argue, what is acceptable – even desirable behaviour – in some computer games is very far from acceptable beyond that imaginary realm, in the lived existence of our daily lives. The influence of violent gaming upon the perceptions of the young and naïve is still under discussion, but it is difficult to assume that it has no influence at all.)

While there is no doubt that the freedom of anonymous, invisible connection via Internet-based conversations offers multiple opportunities for destructive outcomes, this is of course the 'sharp end' of the spectrum of possibilities that the 'brave new world' of virtual communication presents to us. However there are important lessons and challenges here for all virtual communicators about the constant responsibility towards others – their needs and feelings – that working in virtual space entails.

A final word

In this book we have talked about matching the technology to the task at hand, in order to effectively achieve what the client requires – not simply to take the apparently easiest route, or conversely to use a certain technology for a specific outcome simply because it is the latest application or platform. As **Chapter Two** makes clear, the channel of communication needs to match the kind of conversation you wish to have, in order to avoid confusion, misunderstanding and sometimes conflict.

We have also talked about consideration of personal values and expectations, of the impact of communication style, cultural difference, the client's needs and the general 'rules of play' – virtual etiquette, in other words – that all contribute to the kind of atmosphere and mood that you seek to create when working virtually. As stated elsewhere in this book, we find that an approach that includes a regular cycle of respectful and sensitively-delivered feedback in both directions from facilitator to clients during the online sessions is invaluable, as is the responsibility for the facilitator to learn from the feedback, and 'recalibrate' his or her style as appropriate.

But – whether you regard the 'brave new world' of social media and Internet telephony as an enabling and invigorating playground for innovative communication or a mysterious and challenging arena to be entered with fear and reluctance (and we hope not, of course) – it is time for all of us to be aware of, and face up to, some of the trends and questions which we have attempted to explore in this chapter, and throughout this book. Reflecting on these will help us to consider how we each may seek to develop our skills in virtual space, and also help us try to plan a little for what the future may hold.

We will leave it here, and wish you the very best of luck with your explorations in cyber space. We very much hope you will stay in touch with us to share your views and anecdotes.

References

1) Bakas, Adjiedj (2014). Megatrends Werk, Bakas Books BV
2) Caulat, Ghislaine (2006). Virtual Leadership. The Ashridge Journal
3) Cune, Sven and Fogelberg, Fredrik (2011). 'Can remote leadership skills be learnt'; www.nomadicibp.com
4) Cune, Sven and Fogelberg, Fredrik (2012). 'Managing performance remotely'; www.nomadicibp.com
5) Gratton, Lynda (date) The Future of Work is Already Here
6) Gratton, Lynda (2013). HBR webinar
7) Echtelt, P. van (2014). Burn-out: verbanden tussen emotionele uitputting, arbeidsmarktpositie en Het Nieuwe Werken. Den Haag: Sociaal en Cultureel Planbureau.
8) Nyheter, Dagens (2014). Ekonomi
9) Ernst, Chris and Chrobot-Mason, Donna (2011). Boundary Spanning Leadership. McGRaw-Hill
10) Handy, Charles (1993). Understanding Organizations, Penguin
11) Handy, Charles (1995). The Empty Raincoat, Random House
12) Kelley Elizabeth and Kelloway Kevin (2012). Context matters: testing a model of remote leadership; Journal of Leadership & Organisational Studies
13) Meulen, van der Nick, RSM Erasmus University, de staat van het nieuwe werken, Erasmus @ work Research briefing # 6
14) Examples (from Lepsinger, DeRosa (2010). Virtual Team Success)
15) Coleman Parkes Research, amongst 2200 employees across Europe http://www.coleman-parkes.co.uk/
16) Slijkhuis, M. (2012). A structured approach to need for structure at work (proefschrift). Groningen: Rijksuniversiteit Groning
17) Clemons & Kroth (2011). Managing the Mobile Workforce. McGraw-Hill

TOOLBOX SUMMARIES

CHAPTER TWO – *Virtual Communication Technology*

Practical set up considerations

- Use a 'wired' internet connection
- Conduct individual technology checks
- Send a link to a 'test' virtual meeting room
- Include a 'kick off'/initial 'try out' session in your programme or meeting design.

Disaster management and recovery

- Keep the session details handy
- Keep the participant list and e-mail addresses close at hand
- Have a second computer set up
- Consider a second meeting platform
- Have a second producer on hand in case of emergencies.

Choosing your technology platform

- Establish your technology need, using the Task vs. Technology Matrix
- Research the Internet and compare platforms
- Request trial versions for several platforms
- Set up test meetings or pilot training sessions with colleagues or friends in order to experience the level of 'user-friendliness' of the various platforms.

CHAPTER THREE – *The Producer Role*

. . . .

Producer tasks before a session

- Technical checks with participants

- Scheduling sessions

- Sending invitations with joining instructions

- Supporting the facilitator in preparing content and assuring the format is right for virtual delivery.

Producer tasks during a session

- Ensuring a smooth start and entry

- Helping people feel instantly at home

- Helping late attendees to join

- Familiarising participants with the virtual environment

- Supporting guest speakers

- Keeping people busy when something goes wrong

- Managing technical aspects of in-session activities

- Managing time

- Feeding questions to the facilitator or guest speaker

- Communicating with the facilitator 'back stage'.

Producer tasks after a session

- Point of contact for asynchronous activities

- Sending out and collecting evaluations

- Closing a learning programme.

Producer competencies

- Comfortable with Internet technology

- Solution-focused and practical

- Calm and relaxed under pressure

- Excellent communication skills

- Content knowledge about the topic being presented

- Ability to improvise

- Team player – working well with the facilitator

- Versatility and willingness to practise.

CHAPTER FOUR – *Learning Theory and Design of Virtual Events*

Key guidelines

- Any learning and development professional can design a virtual event, but virtual design has some specific characteristics

- Adult learning theory informs us that adults learn by relating new knowledge to existing experience and by application

- Attention span of participants is much shorter in virtual space than in a face to face setting

- Learning in virtual space needs to be much more interactive

- Monologues and lectures should not last longer than 4 minutes

- Decide what needs to be delivered synchronously and what can be done asynchronously

- 'Theoretical' content fits better in an asynchronous than in a synchronous learning environment

- Establishing trust in a group setting enhances learning.

10 Golden rules for virtual design

- Work from the strengths of virtual communication, not its shortcomings

- Interactivity, interactivity, interactivity

- Use features to engage participants

- Address the social aspect of online learning

- Provide structure and clarity

- Apply the rules and principles of virtual etiquette

- Keep sessions short and use energy breaks

- Use virtual breakout rooms in groups of eight or more

- Use images as well as words

- Give opportunities to practise.

CHAPTER FIVE – *Developing Your Own Style and Strengths*

Invite interaction by:

- Asking questions and inviting answers from everyone in the group

- Inviting people to interrupt freely, and to ask questions themselves when they wish

- Inviting people to write responses to questions or comments on your slides or whiteboard

- Inviting people to brainstorm ideas via images or words on a whiteboard

- Organising team games where groups of participants work together

- Inviting people to use the chat-space freely throughout your session

- Setting up small group discussions within the whole group, using breakout room technology for example.

Manage the space around you by:

- Shutting the door of your room and clearing your desk of clutter

- Keeping participants' and your producer's contact details to hand

- Switching your mobile phone off or turn the volume to silent

- Refraining from drinking or eating anything near the mic when live

- Taking notes with pen on paper, or use a computer with a quiet keyboard

- Having the script in front or you (running order; slides) but do not 'read' from it

- Preparing yourself physically to facilitate.

Keep calm by:

- Taking time before the session starts to breathe and calm down

- Having a producer ready to back you up and maintain continuity

- If a problem comes up and affects more than (say) 2 people, informing the group and letting them know that action is being taken

- Having a filler activity or Plan B that the producer and group can use if you need to leave the session or mute yourself

- Breathing and focusing.

Listen well by:

- Being clear it's a conversation, not a monologue, from the outset

- Being inclusive of everyone as much as time allows

- Thanking people for their comments and contributions.

Invite feedback by:

- Using an 'Engagement Barometer' slide or whiteboard

- Inviting people to use the 'emoticons' tools /feedback tools available

- Inviting questions, comments, reactions

- Listening to responses and commenting on these where possible

- Use an online evaluation form at the end of a session.

Combine flexibility and structure by:

- Allowing 'spare' time for flexibility and deviation from the agenda in each session

- Keeping your objectives in mind at all times, and linking any 'spontaneous' contributions to the theme.

Manage time under pressure by:

- Keeping a watch handy at all times

- Being clear about timings for activities.

CHAPTER SIX – *Online Meetings*

Setting up the meeting

- Respect different time zones
- Work from a quiet place
- Notify colleagues and family members that you will be in session
- Ask attendees to attend from their own (not a shared) workstation
- Use a USB headset
- Ensure maximum strength and efficiency from your Internet connection
- If you're using webcam, set the scene a little
- Minimise clutter on your desk.

During the meeting

- Call in early
- Set the scene and run through practicalities
- Explain the process for getting technical support
- Tell people how you want them to communicate with you
- Be clear about how to join and leave the meeting
- Bear in mind language differences and be inclusive
- Balance structure and spontaneity
- Balance getting tasks done with building relationships
- Do a Check In and a Check Out.

Handling Discussions

- Work through the agenda, making sure each point has adequate 'air time'
- Take care to describe each topic or issue

- Invite new information and gather suggestions and solutions from all
- Make sure everyone has a say
- Invite participants to speak, interact and contribute throughout
- Check repeatedly for clarification and invite questions regularly
- Summarise the main information and action points that come out of the discussion
- Begin and end on time.

CHAPTER 7 – *Virtual Communication With Diverse Audiences*

- Include a technology warm-up

- Calmly 'role model' problem-solving behaviour when technical 'glitches' occur

- Create a safe space for people to experiment and learn from mistakes

- Show respect and integrity; encourage regular two-way feedback

- Make virtual facilitation enjoyable, more than 'second-best'

- Be aware of and cater for different personalities and learning styles

- Be ready to work with cultural differences

- Be open and explorative about silence

- Vary the session activities rapidly and frequently

- Explain the rules of communication at the beginning and be assertive about them; use the mute button judiciously

- Respect resistance, check what is causing it, try to resolve it

- Get expectations out in the open and negotiate alternative options

- Have private 1:1 conversations if needed and be careful of over-interpretation

- Realise that learning and behaviour change is also culture change.

CHAPTER 8 – *Cross Cultural Aspects of Virtual Facilitation*

- Make sure you are aware of the cultural background of participants when designing your virtual event

- Map your own culture, and participants' cultures, on the 4 key dimensions discussed, and compare these

- Notice any significant differences between your culture map and those of participants and anticipate how that may affect your session

- Adjust your own communication style to fit the language level and cultural backgrounds of participants

- Select the type of features, interaction, exercises and materials you will use with the 4 key dimensions of culture in mind

- Be informed about the level of proficiency of participants in the language used during the event and adapt your content and approach accordingly

- Anticipate the dynamic between participants from different cultural backgrounds and consider how you will handle any misunderstandings

- Frequently check for understanding in live online events by using annotation features or emoticons

- Avoid humour in diverse groups unless you are 100% sure it is not offensive

- Be prepared for surprises.

CHAPTER 9 – *Getting Organisations Ready for Virtual Communication*

- Consider the introduction of collaborating virtually as (part of) an organisational change project

- Assess the situation and differentiate between working remotely as a goal in itself (with all its benefits) or one of the enablers to reach a 'higher' organisational ambition

- Get a grip on the subject by applying one of the proven frameworks for diagnosing organisational culture and change

- Align the design, tools and implementation of the virtual environment to the type of organisation and its dominant culture

- Consider how the design and use of the virtual environment can help steering the organisation's culture in the required direction

- Apply the success factors for organisational change

- Anticipate the pitfalls of organisational change and prepare to deal with them

- Prepare for, and work with, resistance openly and positively.

RESOURCES

1.1 Definitions of key terms used

Synchronous and Asynchronous Communication

An important distinction is between synchronous and asynchronous ways of working together virtually. By synchronous, we mean that participants join a session simultaneously and communicate in real time by audio, chat, video or screen-sharing. Phone calls and web meetings are examples of synchronous communication.

Asynchronous communication means that people communicate with counterparts while the other person may be offline or even asleep, if in another time zone. The timing of the response depends on the person responding to the message. Email and file sharing are forms of asynchronous communication.

E-learning

E-learning is a form of distance learning where the learner usually sets his or her own pace. Therefore it is asynchronous.

Blended learning is a term used for training programmes where there is a mix of face to face classroom training and self study, by reading, for example.

1.2 Differences and similarities between various types of remote learning

Type	Characteristics	Purpose	Benefits	Disadvantages
E-learning	Asynchronous	Learner can learn at own pace.	Flexibility.	Low engagement.
Remote facilitation	Synchronous	Live connections without travel.	High engagement possible.	All need to join at the same time. Time zone differences may cause inconvenience.
Web meetings	Synchronous	Working together on complex tasks.	High impact meetings.	Familiarity with technology and 'netiquette' required.
Group space	Asynchronous	An Internet-based space for group collaboration.	Fast exchange of information. Builds the team. Defuses conflict.	Difficult to motivate a group to make full use of it.

2.1 Default invitation to virtual event, including asynchronous technology check

Instructions for a Successful Learning Experience in a Virtual Classroom

Preparation

1. Try connecting to this WebEx test meeting to see if your computer is ready to access WebEx. If you cannot access the test meeting, try a different Internet browser.

2. Are you going to join a WebEx session for the first time? Look at this video that explains the basics of WebEx (see link below).

Please take note of the following tips:

1. Ensure you are in front of your own computer, each participant has to log in individually (i.e. not sharing a computer or audio connection with another learner).

2. Work from a quiet space on your own without background noise (i.e. not in a room with other learners).

3. Try to call in 10 minutes before the actual starting time of the session.

4. Use a USB headset for dialing in with your computer OR a telephone with headset for dialing in using your phone (do not use your computer's open speakers or a speaker phone, this can cause audio issues).

5. If you dial in by phone, a landline is preferred.

6. When you try to access a WebEx session for the first time, you might get a request to run or install Java components or to Allow certain exceptions in your firewall. Please click *Yes* or *Allow* when this happens!

7. Please feel free to mute your phone as necessary; however, do not put the call on hold at any time. (If your organization uses background 'hold' music, the entire class will hear it.)

   Wishing you a great virtual session!

2.2 Link to NIBP video 'Intro to the virtual classroom'
A 10 minute introduction for first time participants.
https://www.youtube.com/watch?v=D19l54BoktA

3.1 Excerpt from script for virtual training session – instructions for producer

Timing	Activity	Material	Producer task
Before start	**Virtual Café** • Welcome as participants join • Perform audio check • Set interactive atmosphere.	Slides that stress informality Netiquette Chatbox Whiteboard	Upload documents pre-start Check participants' audio.
00.00	**Welcome and Intro** • Session overview – agenda • Purpose/Objectives of the session • Confidentiality, rules and recording.	Slides	Support participants upon entry.
00.07	**Check-in (with pictures)** • A key characteristic of effective high-performing virtual teams is the balance between task and relationship. • Check In is an activity to bring that balance to the start of a meeting.	Slide with photos of participants and crew	Annotate comments on Check In slide.
00.25	**The virtual classroom environment** A quick tour of the key features and an activity (world map) to practise with the tools.	Slides, Annotation tools, Chat, Emoticons	Explain tools if necessary.

3.2 Excerpt from a Producer Manual for WebEx TC

WebEx host manual

Support participants in joining the audio conference

1. As soon as the participants start joining, greet them by chat and explain that in case of technical issues they can contact you through the chat box.

2. If you see a participant takes a long time to join in the audio conference after he joins in the session, ask if he/she needs help in joining the audio conference.

3. Explain if necessary that participants can join using VOIP or can join using the phone.

4. If a participant wants to call in by phone, he/she needs the right call-in number. This number differs for each location where the participant is calling from. To get an overview of all the call-in numbers, click on 'Session Info' on the top of the WebEx screen, next to 'Quick Start'.

5. Click 'Show all global call-in numbers'. Now you can look up the right number, ask the participants where he/she is calling from.

6. Always stress to the participants the importance of entering the 'Attendee ID number'.

In case of connectivity or audio issues, please refer to the two last paragraphs in this manual.

3.3 Using breakout rooms in your virtual sessions

Setting up and using Breakout Rooms in your Online Meetings

Benefits

Using breakout rooms means that you can assign participants in your meeting to small groups for discussion, brainstorming, reflection – just as you would in face to face training, or in a large-scale meeting or team coaching session. This enables focussed discussion and plenty of interaction and lively debate, even in a large group. It can keep energy and engagement high and increase opportunities for individual learning significantly.

Features

Here are some of the features of Breakout Rooms in Webex.

Privacy: Discussion is entirely private and confidential, which can be a bonus in a large group setting. It is not possible to record the conversations in breakout rooms, only in the plenary.

Document sharing: Slides and whiteboards can be used in the rooms, annotated, saved and shared/debriefed by small groups in the plenary.

Numerous groups can be set up: It is possible to have numerous breakout groups set up, a useful function if you are working with a large group of, say, 100 participants.

Presenter: Each group will automatically have a presenter (who can be assigned in advance) to facilitate the session and keep an eye on time, etc. It is also useful to have a scribe who takes charge of noting comments and saving the whiteboard or slides that are annotated.

Facilitator can enter the sessions to support the groups: Within the Webex set-up it is easy for the main session facilitator and producer to enter the various groups, assist with any problems or questions, and generally keep an eye on time.

Time management: The presenter or producer can enter the group/s to remind them of time, or ask them to return to the plenary. Where time is short, it is also possible to automatically 'close' the sessions so that people are brought back to the main group without being consulted. This may seem 'high control' – it is sometimes necessary to do this under time constraints, however!

Assigning participants to Breakout Sessions

On some platforms (e.g. WebEx and Adobe Connect) it is possible to 'pre-assign' people to breakout rooms before the session starts, or to let the platform automatically do it for you pre-session, or to arrange to do it yourself during the session. We suggest that it is usually helpful to 'pre-assign' participants, as it can take up some valuable time to do it during the session, and you may want to think about who goes in which groups in order to get the best mix of people.

You may also choose to set up the breakout groups during the session itself, by attending people to the groups 'on the spot'. This may work OK in a spontaneous, informal session but takes up lot of time and so may not be a good plan in a more tightly-structured session where the desire is to impress your client.

TIP:

Breakout rooms are not an option to occupy a quick '5 minutes' in your training session or meeting. They take time to set up, and for participants to get in and out smoothly, especially if they are transferring documents from the breakout rooms into the main plenary. We suggest that you do not consider using breakouts unless you have at least 20 minutes for the activity – less time may mean attendees have a rushed discussion and might feel dissatisfied.

4.1 Intake survey for participants in a synchronous learning event

Intake Survey

Please note that individual answers will not be shared.

1. Please state your name:

2. Where are you located?

3. How much of your work takes place virtually?

4. How long have you been leading a remote team?

5. To what extent do you enjoy working virtually?
    a. To a small extent
    b. To a moderate extent
    c. To a large extent
    d. To a very large extent

6. To what extent do you feel you are effective when it comes to working/ leading virtually?
    a. To a small extent
    b. To a moderate extent
    c. To a large extent
    d. To a very large extent

7. What do you see as the benefits of working virtually?

8. What are the main challenges you face working/leading virtually?

9. Which cultures are you in touch with in your team?

10. Which technologies for virtual communication are you using within your team (e.g. Lync)?

11. What are your expectations for this programme?

12. Have you attended any other management training programmes so far? If yes, which ones?

13. Is there anything else you would like to share?

Thank you for filling in the survey!

4.2 Virtual Etiquette or 'Netiquette' – Checklist

Best practices when meeting/communicating virtually

These best practices do not **only** apply to the virtual environment but they **are** especially important when communicating virtually.

In preparation

- **Use a USB headset when using VOIP**
  A headset is always preferred over using speakers. A USB headset will provide the best sound quality.

- **Work from a quiet place**
  You should always try to limit the amount of background noise when you are meeting virtually. Otherwise you'll have to solve this by muting and unmuting when you want to speak up.

- **Notify colleagues in advance you will be in a meeting**
  People generally feel like a virtual meeting is not as important as a face to face meeting. Colleagues therefore might think they can interrupt you when you are in a virtual meeting. By letting your colleagues know in advance, they will not disturb you.

- **Put a sign on your door when in a virtual meeting**
  This will help you to not be interrupted during the meeting.

- **Turn off email, phones, instant messaging tools and clear other distractions away from your desk**
  It's easy to do some other work during a virtual meeting. By clearing all these distractions, you will not be tempted to do this.

- **Pick the right technology**
  Depending on the task at hand you should use different technologies. Some tasks require a lot of social presence, some tasks require a lot of informational richness and some tasks require both. These terms are defined in *Chapter Two*)

- **Have a clear agenda**
  State a clear agenda at the beginning of the meeting. This is important since the time is usually limited when meeting virtually. It is also smart to appoint a meeting leader who keeps track of the agenda.

- **Be prepared**
  Time is usually short when you are meeting virtually. Therefore good preparation is especially important.

During the meeting

- **Call in early**
  Always call in early so you can check if everything works properly. If you experience technical problems, you will then still be able to solve them before the meeting starts.

- **Ensure enough air time for all**
  All participants should get the opportunity to speak up. In an online environment it is too easy for assertive people to 'take over' the meeting discussion time.

- **State your name before you speak**
  When you are with a group of more than five people, it's always a good habit to state your name before you first speak. This way it is always clear who is talking and people soon get to recognise each other's voices.

- **If you leave the meeting, please notify the others**
  If you need to step away from the meeting for a while, always notify the other participants. If you don't respond, others might think you're experiencing technical problems for example, and this can cause concern unnecessarily.

- **Perform a 'Check In' and 'Check Out'.**
  During a Check In all participants share their mood and state their expectations of the meeting. This will help to focus participants on the meeting and also help them engage with each other as a group. During the Check Out participants can state if expectations were met and pick up on anything that hasn't been discussed.

5.1 Virtual goldfish bowl activity

Depending on group size, you may find an exercise like the 'Goldfish bowl' group activity is a preferable alternative to breakout groups, in some instances, for enabling **two groups** to discuss a topic. It also has the benefit of inviting excellent listening and observation skills.

The 'goldfish bowl' activity is so named because it is based on the idea of two groups, one of which is the 'goldfish' in the bowl – a group of people discussing a particular topic or theme set by the facilitator (or considering a case study perhaps). The other group is the 'bowl' – on the 'outside' of the goldfish forming a team of observers.

In virtual space, here's how this works.

1. We use the approach in a group of, say, 12 maximum. In other words, a group that will easily divide into two sub-groups, and where there is not enough time to set up breakout rooms. The benefit of this exercise is that both groups can hear each other's observations in full, pay attention to them, and build on them. This is often a very productive discussion.

2. We might use a slide to show the set up so people understand what is expected of them.

3. We ask the 'goldfish' team going first to spend 10 minutes talking about the particular topic or case study. The 'bowl' team listen with full attention, and quietly. They may choose to open a whiteboard and write their observations and comments so far.

4. After the 10 minutes or so are up, the teams swop around – the 'bowl' team do the talking and the 'goldfish' team become the 'bowl' observers.

5. If notes have been taken on a whiteboard, the second team to talk have something to build on.

Tip: 10 minutes is really a maximum to have one team listening to another, and we would advise less if possible. 5 minutes is probably a minimum to have worthwhile discussion.

6.1 Checklist for preparing virtual meetings

The Big 5: Why, Who, What, How & When
Please fill in the grey colored **text boxes**

● Nomadic
International
Business
Psychology

Why a meeting?

What do you want to achieve?	Make a selection
	If other, specify here
Purpose	Desired end result
	• Sub goal 1
	• Sub goal 2
	• Sub goal 3
Is a meeting the best way to achieve this task?	Keep in mind the task-technology matrix

Who needs to attend?

Number of participants	Insert expected number of participants.
Kind of participants	Choose a participant type.
	Choose a participant type.
	Choose a participant type.
	If other, specify here
Level of meeting techniques	Click to insert text.
Knowledge & expertise on subject	Click to insert text.
Attitude towards subject	Click to insert text.
Personalities & group dynamics	Click to insert text.
Cultural backgrounds	Click to insert text.

What is the content?

Virtual Café *(relationship building)*	Click to insert text.
Check in *(relationship building)*	Click to insert text.
Agenda	• Topic 1
	• Topic 2
	• Topic 3
	• Etc..
Conclusions and Actions	Click to insert text.
Check Out	Click to insert text.

How to achieve this?

Which communication tool is best suited? *(See the Task vs. Technology Matrix on page 2)*	Click to insert text.
What can / needs to be prepared asynchronously?	Click to insert text.
How much time is available?	Total time: Click to insert meeting duration
	Net time:* Click to insert net meeting time
	Total meeting time minus Check In, Check Out and Break time.

Roles	Chair:	Click to insert text.
	Notekeeper:	Click to insert text.
	Producer:	Click to insert text.
	Other:	Click to insert text.
Which facilitation style is best suited?	Click to insert text.	
What kind of contribution is expected from participants?	Click to insert text.	
How will decisions be made?	Choose a decision process	
	If other, specify here	
How will action items be recorded and distributed?	Click to insert text.	

Keep in mind

- Select a time that is reasonable for all time zones or rotate the inconvenient hours: http://www.timeanddate.com/worldclock/meeting.html
- Select a technology to which all have access and with which are all familiar.
- Balance task and relationship – 'task focus' only sets the team up for failure
- Agenda items should be all participants' business – if an item is only 2 or 3 people's business, deal with it offline
- Invite only those who are needed
- Meetings longer than 2 hours are ineffective
- Create engagement; do not broadcast but ask questions
- Take a short break after 1 hour in a conference call or web meeting
- Send invitation with purpose (why), agenda (what), participant list (who) and process (how)

Task-Technology Matrix

	Exchanging information	Producing documents	Explaining/ having difficult conversations	Brainstorming and discussing	Building relationships
Email	🙂	🙂	🙁	🙁	😐
Text message	🙂	🙁	🙁	🙁	🙂
Chat	🙂	😐	😐	😐	🙂
Phone	🙂	🙁	😐	🙂	🙂
Phone conference	🙁	🙁	😐	😐	😐
Video conference	🙁	😐	🙂	🙂	🙂
Video conference 2.0 (Halo/Telepresence)	🙁	🙂	🙂	🙂	🙂
Web meeting platform	🙁	🙂	🙂	🙂	🙂

6.2 Decision-making tool 'Fist to Five'

A decision-making tool aimed at reaching team consensus

Source: Rindone, N. K. (1996). Effective Teaming for Success. Presented at the workshop for the Kansas State Department of Education, Students Support Services, Boots Adams Alumni Center, University of Kansas, Lawrence, Kansas

A decision-making technique that works very well online is the Fist to Five decision-making process. The five options when voting on a topic are the following:

Fist   I can't live with the decision; I will block it or leave the group.

One   I don't like it but I won't block it. Don't count on me for a lot of energy.

Two   I'm not excited by the decision, but I will do some work to support it.

Three   I think the decision is okay; I will get involved.

Four   I think the decision is good; I will work hard to support it.

Five   I think the decision is great; I may leave the group if it is not made.

It is a powerful tool as it forces each participant to take a stand on each topic, but at the same time it gives room for expressing how much you are opposed or in favour of an idea/solution.

Other ways of decision-making are through consensus, or by voting where the majority rules. Both options have their advantages and disadvantages. Looking for consensus can take a long time (or might be impossible), but, if consensus is won, it means all participants are likely to commit to decision and work hard for it. Majority rules decision-making can be done quickly but it promotes a win-lose dynamic in the group and this can be very demotivating and unproductive in the long run.

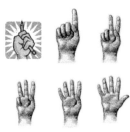

7.1 How to give feedback

How to give feedback

Source: Centre for Creative Leadership www.ccl.org

- Check out 'Why do I want to give this feedback?'

- Talk about issues over which the individual has some control

- Give both positive and critical feedback, but tip the balance in the positive direction. Use the 4:1 rule as a guide

- Report on specific, observable behaviour, rather than on conclusions you draw from the behaviour

- Give examples

- Don't psychoanalyse; avoid inferences and interpretations

- Avoid loaded terms and inflammatory labels

- Ensure the feedback is non-evaluative. Identify opinions, perceptions, and reactions as different from facts

- Communicate acceptance of the person receiving feedback

- Be honest, kind, sincere, and warm – make your feedback a gift

- Allow time for clarification. Provide an opportunity for the individual to react

- If requested, identify ways to improve performance.

7.2 The SBI feedback model (Source: Centre for Creative Leadership)

Situation:

- The specific event or circumstance.

Behavior is:

- Observable actions

- Verbal comments

- Nonverbal behaviours and signals

- Mannerisms.

Impact is:

- What I (or others) think, feel, or do as a result

- I saw ... I heard ... I felt ... I thought ...

- It is not an interpretation or judgment on motivation or intent.

(Source: Centre for Creative Leadership www.ccl.org)

8.1. Balancing transparency and relationship focus in email messages

Delegates in a training programme from Worldwork (www.worldwork.biz) were asked to write an e-mail giving feedback to a fellow member of their project team. The instruction was that the team member had not delivered as promised and this was having a negative impact on the project.

Here are 3 versions of the same message: a low context message, a high context message and a message that balances task and relationship focus.

Email #1 (low context)

Subject: problem with unmet criteria

Dear…,

I'm very rushed, so I need to keep the information very short and direct. I'm sorry, but I'm very disappointed and unsatisfied with the way you are working on this project. It does not meet at all the criteria we agreed upon from the start. You really need to do this in a much more professional way and according to our goals and criteria. Otherwise we really have a problem. I suggest that we will have a talk tomorrow. Then I will explain clearly what I mean. Speak to you tomorrow at 14.00.

Email #2 (high context)

Subject: a new beginning together

Hello

I'm glad to write you this email and I'd like to thank you for your hard work. As you know we will work together. You know it's an important time now at the beginning of the project, so we can share some information to improve our work. I hope we will have a good time in working.

I'm sure we will have a new beginning through our common effort.

This is my telephone number…if you have any time to talk about some things.

Best regards

Sample # 3 (balancing the relationship focus with transparency)

Dear...

I hope all of you are also holding up under the project stress over there. This is a big opportunity for our company and we will make it for sure. RAPPORT ('WE') WITH TRANSPARENCY

I just want to mention again the request (my last mail from Aug 2) regarding the...data. We would really need this very soon as your input is crucial in our process chain, especially as the programmers need to have everybody's data. TRANSPARENCY (WITH REASON FOR NEED)

We are all facing challenges with multiple deadlines, nevertheless could you please let me know when we will receive your input? RAPPORT/TRANSPARENCY

Perhaps we could talk on the phone later today to catch up where we all are on the project as a whole. RAPPORT WITH CLEAR INTENTION

Do let me know a good time for you.

Thanks

(Source: Worldwork www.worldwork.biz)

Printed in Great Britain
by Amazon